006.33. 0000097

An Introduction to Expert Systems

An Introduction to Expert Systems

Michel Gondran
Translated from the French by
Joanna Gosling
English edition prepared by
Peter Gosling

McGRAW-HILL Book Company (UK) Limited

London · New York · St Louis · San Francisco · Auckland · Bogotá
Guatemala · Hamburg · Johannesburg · Lisbon · Madrid
Mexico · Montreal · New Delhi · Panama · Paris · San Juan
São Paulo · Singapore · Sydney · Tokyo · Toronto

Published by
McGRAW-HILL Book Company (UK) Limited
MAIDENHEAD · BERKSHIRE · ENGLAND

British Library Cataloguing in Publication Data
Gondran, Michel
An introduction to expert systems.
1. Expert systems (Computer science)
I. Title II. Introduction aux systèmes expertes. *English*
006.3'3   QA76.9.E96

ISBN 0-07-084920-X

Library of Congress Cataloging-in-Publication Data
Gondran, Michel.
An introduction to expert systems.

Translation of: Introduction aux systèmes experts.
Bibliography: p.
1. Expert systems (Computer science) I. Title.
QA76.76.E95G6613   1986   006.3'3   85-23696
ISBN 0-07-084920-X

First published by Edition Eyrolles, Paris
First edition © Edition Eyrolles, 1983

12345 WL 89876

Typeset by Eta Services (Typesetters) Ltd., Beccles, Suffolk and printed and bound in
Great Britain by Whitstable Litho Limited, Whitstable, Kent

Contents

Acknowledgement

Grateful thanks to Kevin Hughes, Simon Parry, and Mike Barrett of Expertech Research Limited for their help in the preparation of the English edition.

1. Introduction

The goal of an artificial intelligence system is to analyse human behaviour in the fields of perception, comprehension, and decision making in the ultimate hope of reproducing them on a machine, namely a computer.

An expert system is the first true operational application of this type of research and this book aims to present the basic structure of an expert system in a simple form and to point towards its future development.

As an introduction we will specify the place of expert systems in the field of artificial intelligence. In Chapter 2 we will describe the general principles behind such systems by means of a few examples which serve as their foundation.

Chapter 3 is a short introduction to the role of artificial knowledge in the development of expert systems and in Chapter 4 we present an objective account of the SNARK language developed by J. L. Laurière. It would appear that SNARK currently forms the basis of many projected expert systems. Four examples are presented in this chapter as illustrations of the use of this technique.

Then in Chapter 5 the algorithm for an expert system is developed in more detail, while Chapter 6 describes several applications of expert systems.

Chapter 7 is devoted to a survey of the future role of expert systems.

1.1 Artificial intelligence

The study of artificial intelligence (AI) concerns all those activities of man for which there are no set procedures laid down. If computer science is the science of information processing by a set algorithmic approach then the study of AI looks at all those activities which cannot be treated at a simple, standard, algorithmic level.

There are so many activities, even in trivial situations such as reading a book or an article, where what we do and how we do it is not governed by a set of well-defined rules. For example, a character such as '!' can be interpreted, according to its context, by our visual system sometimes as an 'i', sometimes as an 'l' or even as a specially defined character. In the case of handwriting things are even worse. The following three words all start with the same graphic symbol *n*, but because of its context it becomes endowed with three quite different meanings: *notive, note, ntility.* How does our cognitive system remove these ambiguities? This is just one of the problems highlighted in the study of AI.

The traditional programming languages do not allow us to communicate with the computer in anything but an algorithmic manner by issuing a series of orders. In AI, heuristics, or rules of thumb, are substituted for algorithms.

These rules of thumb should take account of the characteristics of the particular problem being studied. They consider not only the data but also its context.

Let us consider the way we perform the task of adding two numbers together. If the numbers are very small, say less than 20, we will often obtain the result by 'fusing' the two numbers together. If the numbers are larger than about 20 then we may have to perform a more complicated operation using 'carrying' figures in our head. If the numbers are too big to add together in this way then we may have to write the entire sum down on paper. This is a case where we do not always carry out the operation in the same manner every time. The method we employ depends on the data we are handling.

The earliest research into AI often had goals which were overambitious. The researchers could see that what they were doing had applications in a vast number of different areas, but their hopes rested on an underestimation of the size of the problems which had first of all to be solved before a practical system could be evolved. Automatic language translation programs were an early example of this situation.

Work on automatic translation began in the fifties. Each word in a group had a set of alternative translations and simple rules were established in order to put the appropriate translated words into a sensible order and to improve syntax. This highly syntactic approach produced some terrible blunders. For example, when the English sentence 'The spirit is willing, but the flesh is weak' was translated into Russian and then back into English again it emerged as 'Vodka is strong, but meat is rotten'.

Work on artificial translation was almost totally abandoned in the mid-sixties as the result of the ALPAC report which had been commissioned to evaluate the project. The report came to the conclusion that a suitable system was impossible to devise.

You have therefore to go via the meaning of the text in order to be able to translate it properly and you must not be taken in, as so many people were in 1966, by the ELIZA program of J. Weizenbaum. This program short-circuits real linguistic processes and uses a clever system of models with fixed answers which mimic language in a very convincing way. The program responses imitate those of a psychiatrist. Each response is drawn from a series of sentences or phrases which are kept in the memory and are triggered off by certain words, or words belonging to a certain group, which appear in the sentences typed in by the 'patient'. For example, each time the word 'mother' is mentioned the program produces the response of the following type, 'Tell me about your mother'. If you type in 'I feel a little tired', ELIZA uses part of the patient's sentence in its reply, 'Why are you feeling a little tired?'.

Weizenbaum realized, as a result, that this program showed how dangerous it was to take the simulation of human behaviour as a gauge with which to measure the 'intelligence' of a computer. He noticed that ELIZA operated at a very simple and superficial level of language comprehension and that, in spite of this, some people were fooled by the apparent reality of the responses to the point where they were confiding their personal problems to the computer as if it really were a psychiatrist.

The most important developments in AI were made on problem solving and were centred on the intelligent discovery of solutions thanks to the rules of thumb which had been given to the machine. As examples, see the GENERAL PROBLEM SOLVER program by A. Newall and H. Simon (Nobel Prize for Economics, 1978) and the ALICE program of J. L. Laurière (European Research Prize CII-HB, 1982).

1.2 Expert systems

For several years now researchers have noticed that one essential element was missing from all the existing programs. It was that there seemed to be a lack of in-depth knowledge of the area which is being dealt with at any time. In other words, there was none of the cumulative knowledge which comes from years of practice and experience. This cumulative knowledge comes from making analogies, relating pieces of information, and possessing significant amounts of knowledge in a wide variety of fields.

Information which is simply stored in a database is easy to extract. What is difficult is to deduce the facts which have not been recorded in the database but could be deduced from the stored information.

The aim of an expert system is to reproduce the behaviour of a human expert, thus performing an intellectual task in a specific field. Expert systems position themselves at the junction of the two approaches to AI; the representation of information on the one hand and its automatic 'demonstration' on the other.

These form two totally independent systems:

– a knowledge base,
– a 'demonstrator' of theorems (an 'inference engine' or rule interpreter).

The knowledge base translates expert knowledge in a given field into a declaratory and modular form. The 'demonstrator' has the task of calling up and using this information in a meaningful way in order to answer a question or solve a problem.

An expert system differs from a conventional computer program in two essential ways since at any time an expert system can:

- explain its behaviour to the human expert,
- receive new pieces of information from the human expert without any new programming being required.

The knowledge base must be readable on its own and must exist independently from the 'inference engine', but must be capable of being interpreted by it, and this knowledge base must be under the control of the human expert.

2. How to structure the base of an expert system

2.1 Schema of an expert system

Language is the most general current representation of information. It may be broken down into sentences which form blocks or modules of information. Expert systems use this modular approach to the structure of information.

In the case of most expert systems the information used will be one of two types. One is a base of facts and the other is a base of rules of production of these facts. It is this type of expert system we will deal with in this book. Other representations are covered by Schank (1977), Charniak (1978), Codier (1979), and Pastre (1978).

Example 1

Let us consider the following knowledge base:

Initial base of facts: H,K

Base of rules: (R1) $A \rightarrow E$
(R2) $B \rightarrow D$
(R3) $H \rightarrow A$
(R4) $E \text{ and } G \rightarrow C$
(R5) $E \text{ and } K \rightarrow B$
(R6) $D \text{ and } E \text{ and } K \rightarrow C$
(R7) $G \text{ and } K \text{ and } F \rightarrow A$

where $A \rightarrow E$ means 'E may be deduced from A'.

The inference engine induces from the facts contained in the knowledge base and uses the rule of *modus ponens* which is the rule that 'if P is true and if $P \rightarrow Q$ then Q must be true'.

Two general strategies of demonstration are therefore possible:

1. *Forward chaining* Start from the original base of facts and trigger off the rules for which the premises on the left-hand side are satisfied. Add to this the facts which are obtained in this way and continue until 'saturation point' is reached.

In Example 1 a chain is obtained from the following derivation:

$$
\begin{array}{ll}
\text{H} \rightarrow \text{A} \quad (\text{R3}) & (\text{base of facts} = \{\text{A, H, K}\} \\
\text{A} \rightarrow \text{E} \quad (\text{R1}) & \{\text{A, E, H, K}\} \\
\text{E and K} \rightarrow \text{B} \quad (\text{R5}) & \{\text{A, B, E, H, K}\} \\
\text{B} \rightarrow \text{D} \quad (\text{R2}) & \{\text{A, B, D, E, H, K}\} \\
\text{D and E and K} \rightarrow \text{C} \quad (\text{R6}) & \{\text{A, B, C, D, E, H, K}\}
\end{array}
$$

2. *Backward chaining* If your aim is to show that fact D is correct then you look at all the rules which have that aim on the right-hand side. Each of these rules is then considered and if all the premises have been satisfied in the original base of facts then you have reached your goal; otherwise the unknown premises are recorded as if they were new aims and you begin the cycle again for each of them.

In Example 1 the rule R2 is considered and B is defined as a new goal. Then rule R5 is considered and E is defined as a new goal. Then rule R1 is considered and A is defined as a new goal. Then rules R3 and R7 are considered and it is R3 which provides the conclusion. We have been led backwards through rules R2, R5, R1, and R3 to the two things we do know, which are H and K. The pursuit of a goal is usually represented by means of an AND/OR tree, and in this case the tree would be as shown in Fig. 2.1.

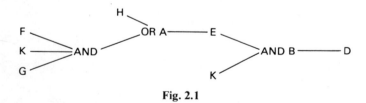

Fig. 2.1

Note 1: The forward chaining strategy is used in the SNARK inference engine (Laurière, 1982c), and the backward chaining in the EMYCIN inference engine (Van Melle, 1979).

Example 2

This comes from the field of botany and we will look at the base of rules which follow. In this the proposition 'plants have a flower' is abbreviated to 'flower'. The $\wedge$ symbol corresponds to the logical connector 'and' and the $\neg$ symbol corresponds to negation.

(a) IF flower $\wedge$ seed THEN phanerogam
(b) IF phanerogam $\wedge$ unprotected seed THEN fir tree

(c) IF phanerogam ∧ 1-cotyledon THEN monocotyledon
(d) IF phanerogam ∧ 2-cotyledons THEN dicotyledon
(e) IF monocotyledon ∧ rhizome THEN lily of the valley
(f) IF dicotyledon THEN anemone
(g) IF monocotyledon ∧ (¬ rhizome) THEN lilac
(h) IF leaf ∧ flower THEN cryptogam
(i) IF cryptogam ∧ (¬ root) THEN moss
(j) IF cryptogam ∧ root THEN fern
(k) IF (¬ leaves) ∧ plant THEN thallophyte
(l) IF thallophyte ∧ chlorophyll THEN algae
(m) IF thallophyte ∧ (¬ chlorophyll) THEN mushroom
(n) IF (¬ leaf) ∧ (¬ flower) ∧ (¬ plant) THEN colon bacillus

Thus (a) means that 'IF the plant has a flower and a seed THEN the plant has a phanerogam'.

The problem we are faced with is to determine what the plant is which has the following characteristics: rhizome, flower, seed, 1-cotyledon. This forms our current base of facts. If we use forward chaining we get the following derivation:

(a) → phanerogam
(c) → monocotyledon
(e) → lily of the valley

and these are the only rules we use in this case to obtain the solution 'lily of the valley'.

As a result the facts and the rules of production must be more closely defined.

Fundamentally, two types of production rules are used. One is based on propositional logic and the other on first-order logic.

2.2 First-order logic

Examples 1 and 2 represent typical cases of propositional logic. The rules apply directly to the facts, i.e., the premises and consequences of the rules are explicitly the facts. On the other hand, the rules which are based on first-order logic can use variables and quantifiers and can also be applied to a whole class of facts.

As a result, rules may be introduced such as:

IF man (x) THEN mortal (x)

which means: 'If x is a man THEN x is a mortal'. The well-known syllogism which is generally attributed to Aristotle:

All men are mortals,
Socrates is a man,
Therefore Socrates is mortal.

which can be described as follows:

The initial base of facts: man (Socrates)
(which means 'Socrates is a man')

The initial base of rules: IF man (x) THEN mortal (x)
(which means 'men are mortal')

Therefore the following fact may be deduced:
mortal (Socrates)

You will notice that, in this case, in order to apply the rule you must look at the base of facts for a man which will allow you to particularize the variable x. Another interesting example is the possibility of using theorems such as those of transitivity which can be represented by the following rules:

IF element (y) = x
and element (z) = y
THEN element (z) = x

(which means 'IF x is an element of y and if y is an element of z THEN x is an element of z').

So, from the fact that the tyre is an element of the wheel (element (wheel) = tyre) and that the wheel is an element of the bicycle (element (bicycle) = wheel), the rule of transitivity allows the system the knowledge that the tyre is an element of the bicycle (element (bicycle) = tyre).

This very general rule allows us to state an important piece of information in an implicit way.

Another example of a rule of first-order logic is:

IF father (x) = y
   mother (y) = z
THEN grandmother (x) = z

(which means 'if y is the father of x and z is the mother of y, then z is the grandmother of x').

Here are two more examples taken from *La Logigue sans peine* by Lewis Carroll (*Symbolic Logic*, 1896) which illustrate a number of useful points.

Example 3

1. Babies are illogical.
2. Never despise the man who can stand at arm's length from a crocodile.
3. Illogical people are despised.

Come to a conclusion about these statements.

Let us translate these three statements into the language of first-order logic.

1. $\neg$ logical (babies)
2. IF stand at arm's length from a crocodile (x) THEN $\neg$ despised (x)
3. IF $\neg$ logical (x) THEN despised (x)

(where statement 3, for example, means 'If x is illogical, then x is despised').

Statement 1 makes up the base of facts. Statements 2 and 3 make up the base of rules.

Using statements 1 and 3 we can deduce that

despised (babies)

which mean 'babies are despised'. Then we can go no further.

However, there is a classic result which occurs in the theory of groups which allows us to write the rule 'IF A THEN B' in the equivalent form of 'IF B THEN A'. This means that we can write statements 2 and 3 as:

2a. IF despised (x) THEN $\neg$ stand at arm's length from a crocodile (x)
3a. IF $\neg$ despised (x) THEN logical (x)

The base of rules is now 2, 2a, 3, and 3a. In using 1, 3, and 2a in succession we may come to the conclusion that:

$\neg$ stand at arm's length from a crocodile (babies)

(which means 'babies cannot stand at arm's length from crocodiles').

Note 2: Even in a simple example the transformation into first-order logic is not completely 'trivial'. In order to be able to use forward chaining for deductions we are forced in this case to represent each statement in one of two ways (2 and 2a, 3 and 3a).

Example 4

1. Animals are always mortally offended if I take no notice of them.
2. The only animals which belong to me are in this meadow.
3. No animal is able to solve a riddle if he has received no suitable education.
4. None of the animals in this meadow are water rats.
5. When an animal is mortally offended it always starts to run about and scream.

6. I never pay attention to an animal which does not belong to me.
7. No animal which has received suitable education starts to run about and scream.

Find a conclusion to these seven statements.

First of all we will translate these statements using first-order logic. The variable x in this case applies to 'animal'.

1. IF ￢ attention (x) THEN mortally offended (x)
2. IF ￢ meadow (x) THEN ￢ belongs to (x)
3. IF ￢ education (x) THEN ￢ solve riddle (x)
4. ￢ meadow (water rat)
5. IF mortally offended (x) THEN runs and screams (x)
6. IF ￢ belongs to (x) THEN ￢ attention (x)
7. IF runs and screams (x) THEN ￢ education (x)

Statement 4 makes up the base of facts. The others make up the base of rules.

We can make a simple deduction by using statements 4, 2, 6, 1, 5, 7, and 3 in that order in order to deduce that 'no water rat is able to solve a riddle'.

Note 3: You can already notice a slight difference between databases. In the case of the databases used in data processing it is the knowledge of facts which represents virtually the sum total of the knowledge. With expert systems it is the base of rules which represent virtually the sum total of the knowledge. In the case of a diagnosis problem, the base of facts is only concerned with the data which is relative to the current situation. For a medical diagnosis this would be the data which is provided by a particular patient. For the diagnosis of an 'incident' the data would have been provided by different witnesses.

The use of propositions in expert systems does not lend itself to constructing wide-ranging and extensive systems.

Systems of the future will be based on first-order logic, cf. OPS, SNARK (Laurière, 1982c), PROLOG (Colmerauer, 1977), TANGO (Cordier and Rousset, 1982), ALOUETTE (Mulet-Marquis, 1983).

2.3 The inference engine

Let us consider the case of forward chaining. Our inference engine knows on the one hand the order in which it will try to apply the rules and on the other hand the order in which they will actually be applied.

In the case of most existing expert systems (cf. PROSPECTOR systems (Konolige, 1979), SAM (Gascuel, 1981), and the systems based on PRO-

LOG), the order in which the rules are tried is static. This approach is of use while there is a natural order of rules in existence. Likewise, in Example 4, two types of graph can be defined which represent a total order for the statements or possible facts (see Fig. 2.2) and a total order for the rules (see Fig. 2.3).

Fig. 2.2   Order of possible facts in Example 4

Fig. 2.3   Order for the rules in Example 4

As in Example 1 one is able to define two types of graph. The first of these is the graph of the precedence of possible facts when fact i precedes fact j as a result (see Fig. 2.4). The second is the graph for the precedence of rules when rule k precedes rule l (the arc k, l) if, within the results of rule k, a fact exists which may be within the premises of rule l (see Fig. 2.5).

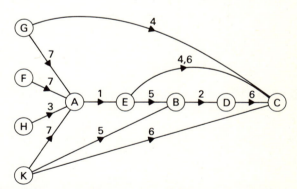

Fig. 2.4   Graph for the order of precedence of the facts in Example 1

You should notice that the arcs in the graph for precedence of possible facts may be labelled with the rules and that the arcs of the graph for the precedence of rules may be labelled with the facts.

The graph for precedence of rules in Example 1 was without a circuit, so

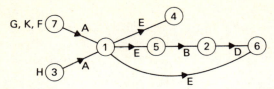

Fig. 2.5 Graph for the order of precedence of the rules in Example 1

you can choose a total order for the rules compatible with the partial order 7, 3, 1, 4, 5, 2, 6, and this is the method of approach chosen for **PROSPECTOR**. You could, however, come to a satisfactory static order for the rules by minimizing the number of returning arcs (see the problem of the partial circuitless graph in Gondran and Minoux, 1979, p. 372).

The safest approach, but one which has a far more complicated method of application, is to find a dynamic order which is dependent on context. This is the methodology used in SNARK (Laurière, 1982c) and ALOUETTE (Mulet-Marquis, 1983, [cf. Chapter 5, Sec. 5.2]).

3. Representation of knowledge and metaknowledge

The system described in the previous chapter is a very formal system based uniquely on logic. However, if the knowledge base is both quantitatively and qualitatively important then an expert system of this type turns out to be very useful. In Chapter 4 we will show the construction of a base of information as used by the SNARK system.

Schematically we must resolve a problem in three stages. These are the understanding of the terms, the search for a good representation of the problem, and deciding on a method to solve the problem. These three stages are not independent of each other and can often be confused.

3.1 Understanding the terms

The first part of this stage corresponds in AI to the research which has been carried out on the comprehension of natural language. The earliest studies were based substantially on a syntactic analysis of sentences by word-by-word study. Chomsky's syntactic grammars were used (1965) and these were represented by the rules of formal transformational grammar.

The need soon arose for these relative ambiguities to be suitably resolved, such as those found in the case of pronouns, for example, where you have temporarily to suspend the sentence analysis process at a given level in order to descend to a lower level to study a connected preposition before returning to the analysis. For this analysis, which is both semantic and syntactic, transition networks are currently being used, or even augmented transition networks (ATN) as introduced by Woods in 1970.

This approach is practical within the limited fields where transition networks have already been defined. It could be extended into other fields by the construction of ATN.

Insofar as a text is recognized by such systems it is translated into an internal representation called a 'semantic network' which connects particular pieces of information in the text to be studied (see Simmons, 1973, and

Cordier, 1979). The network, initially empty, is continually added to, modified, and corrected during the course of the analysis. It can store certain pieces of information, even information which is simply probable or conditional.

The phrase 'understanding of terms' is not quite so simple for us to understand as it appears. It is suggested that you attempt a few of the following games of logic which have been taken from *Jouer à Raisonner* (Dumont and Schuster, 1982). When you have read each of the texts answer each of the questions. Answer TRUE if it is obviously affirmed within the text. Answer FALSE if the opposite is true. Select ARGUABLE if you are not sure whether it is true or false. Consult the text as often as you like. Allow yourself two minutes per question.

3.1.1 Theft in the dark

There were no customers in the branch of the Daissoux Bank which is at 36a Avenue Arpagon. The employees (all of them men, for this company is exceedingly mysogynist) were attending to current business. A man came in followed by two blind people. One of the two blind people went up to the tills, the other went towards the cash desk. The cashier was surprised to notice that the pseudo-blind person did not need his glasses in order to aim properly. Six months later Inspector Lapreuve arrested all of these criminals. The search which was carried out at their home led to the discovery of a large sum of money.

Questions	YES	NO	?
1. The two blind people stole a large amount of money.			
2. The money from the robbery was not found.			
3. The cashier was wounded.			
4. All the characters in the story are men.			
5. The two blind people were arrested.			
6. The Daissoux Bank has a branch in Avenue Arpagon.			
7. One of the blind people was a good shot.			
8. At the start of the action there were no customers.			
9. Lapreuve arrested two criminals six months later.			
10. The story does not give the age of the cashier.			

3.1.2 The till money

The last customer had just left the shop. One of the owners was collecting up the contents of the till when a man entered. The stranger went straight to the manager and demanded some money. The light suddenly went out. When it came on again the stranger had disappeared. All the tills were empty. Inspector Lapreuve, informed of the incident, arrived immediately.

Questions	YES	NO	?
1. The stranger spoke to the manager.			
2. The thief did not ask for any money.			
3. There was only one owner.			
4. The thief cut off the electricity.			
5. The story does not specify how much money disappeared.			
6. There were only two people present when the man came in.			
7. The thief wanted some money.			
8. The manager was collecting up the contents of the till.			
9. The owner recognized the stranger.			
10. Inspector Lapreuve was looking for the stranger.			

3.1.3 Who killed the spy?

Our spy had an unfortunate accident at work. His body had been discovered in a public park. The murderer had no doubt in his mind. Inspector Lapreuve had three notorious spies arrested who lived close to the park. On questioning all the suspects Lapreuve dismissed Leopold Van Deboutt (called 'the Swiss') who was at the Lichtenstein Embassy at the estimated time of the murder.

Questions

	YES	NO	?
1. The spy was murdered.			
2. The murder took place in a public park.			
3. Three suspects live quite close to the crime.			
4. Leopold is a spy.			
5. Lapreuve arrested three suspects.			
6. Leopold was Swiss.			
7. Leopold was dismissed.			
8. Lapreuve knows who killed the spy.			
9. All the suspects were interrogated.			
10. The spy was Chinese.			

3.1.4 Answering the questions

Here is how a perfect witness would answer the questions:

Theft in the dark

1. ?... Only one of the suspects is likely to be responsible.
2. ?... The money which was found probably came from the other hold-ups.
3. ?... If the cashier states that the blind person was a good shot he was not necessarily wounded.
4. ?... A blind person could be female.
5. ?... See 1.
6. Yes.
7. Yes.
8. Yes.
9. ?... It is not specified how many there are of them. There could have been three of them; the two blind people and the man who preceded them.
10. Yes.

The till money

1. Yes.

2. ?... We do not know whether the stranger is the thief or even if there was a theft.
3. No. '... one of the owners....'.
4. ?... See 2.
5. ?... See 2.
6. ?... There is at least one owner and one manager, but there possibly could be a cleaning lady.
7. ?
8. ?
9. ?
10. ?

Who killed the spy?

1. Yes. 'The murderer had no doubt in his mind.'
2. ?... The murder could have happened elsewhere and the body could have been taken to the park to be hidden.
3. ?... Idem.
4. ?... The three spies were not necessarily the only suspects.
5. No. 'Lapreueve had *them* arrested....'
6. ?... He called himself 'the Swiss'.
7. Yes.
8. ?... Nothing is said on this subject.
9. Yes.
10. ?

The interpretation of the numerous errors in spite of the apparent simplicity of the text is really quite interesting. It shows how the imagination can work on the construction of a description (see Fig. 3.1). The texts we studied are full of loopholes and the imagination automatically pounces on them. The imaginary description is built up and links are invented between the gaps in the text. The elements of the story are thus interwoven and rearranged according to the structure we think is most likely. The reconstruction is made up by an inductive process and as this reconstruction is unaware of this the induction is often somewhat weird and incorrect.

The comparison of your replies with those of a colleague could not fail to be enlightening. People often justify their mistakes under the pretext that anybody would fall into them in the same way. So it is constructive to state that mistakes differ from person to person while each person is strongly convinced that they personally found the correct solution! In fact, imagination works for each of us in a different way. It works haphazardly, inventing new text for itself. Even facts which are solidly fixed in the original story are often

Fig. 3.1 The brain and thought have always encouraged artistic interpretation. On this seventeenth century drawing Robert Fludd tried to represent the complexity of the cerebral system. (The illustration is taken from *The Illustrated History of the Functions of the Brain* by Edwin Clarke, Kenneth Dewhurst, and Dacosta.)

rejected in the final description if they no longer fit in with the new elements you have invented! The description appears to have taken place in reality!

This phenomenon of completion by imagination differs according to the individual and is almost certainly at the base of numerous misunderstandings between people who in fact think they are talking about the same thing.

3.2 Representation of information

The role of description is equally essential in the domain of understanding a problem as in solving it. Likewise, if we return to Examples 2 and 3 in

Chapter 2 the representation of the original text by means of the rules of first-order logic allows us to come to the right conclusions without difficulty.

Here are two examples which demonstrate the essential role of the representation of information. First of all we have a little logic puzzle.

Example 5: Choose your flower

Alan, Eric, Patrick, Daniel, and John go collecting mountain flowers. They choose Bavarian gentian, arnica, rhododendron, edelweiss, and blue thistles and they decide that no one is to collect more than one sort of flower.

The boy who is looking for arnica and the boy who is looking for rhododendron advise Alan to put his flowers into a plastic bag as they will wilt very quickly.

John wants to keep his flowers fresh, while the boy who is looking for edelweiss and Eric want to dry theirs.

John and the boy who is collecting rhododendron fear that they will have trouble, for the plants they are hunting are beginning to lose their flowers. On the other hand, the blue thistle is just beginning to go brown.

Alan and Daniel advise the boy who is looking for edelweiss and the boy who is looking for blue thistles to try not to collect too much as they are particularly rare.

Which flower did each boy choose?

The question concerns the relationship between the boys and the flowers. So we must limit ourselves. First of all we should only write down the information concerning the boy–flower relationship. From the sentence which says 'The boy who is looking for arnica and the boy who is looking for rhododendron advise Alan to put his flowers into a plastic bag as they will wilt very quickly' you only need to retain the information that can be translated into a first-order logic statement as:

$\neg$ collects (Alan) = arnica, rhododendron

and for the other statements we can write:

$\neg$ collects (John) = edelweiss
$\neg$ collects (Eric) = edelweiss
$\neg$ collects (John) = rhododendron
$\neg$ collects (Alan) = edelweiss, blue thistles
$\neg$ collects (Daniel) = edelweiss, blue thistles

From this representation of the information (having made up groups for John and Alan) we can easily work out the solution to the problem.

In the same way, there is only one link which comes into play, the link $\neg$

collects. This link can be represented by the following table where the crosses indicate the impossibilities:

	Alan	Eric	Patrick	Daniel	John
Bavarian gentian					
Arnica	X				
Rhododendron	X				X
Edelweiss	X	X		X	X
Blue thistle	X			X	X

From this we can deduce, in order, that

collects (Alan) = Bavarian gentian

so that

collects (John) = Bavarian gentian

from which we get

collects (John) = arnica

and so on. The end result becomes:

	Alan	Eric	Patrick	Daniel	John
Bavarian gentian	OK	X	X	X	X
Arnica	X	X	X	X	OK
Rhododendron	X	X	X	OK	X
Edelweiss	X	X	OK	X	X
Blue thistle	X	OK	X	X	X

Example 6: Instant insanity (Laurière, 1979)

Having been given four cubes of which the sides have been painted either in red (R), yellow (Y), blue (B), or green (G) according to Fig. 3.2, you must now stack them up in order to make a parallelopiped which has to show each of the four colours on each of its main sides. The Miro Company invented this puzzle and named it 'Instant insanity'.

Our eyes and hands are quite used to working together as a team in mid-air. It is therefore easy for us to put the cubes one on top of the other and to turn them round. However, to do this in the third dimension is not easy. We

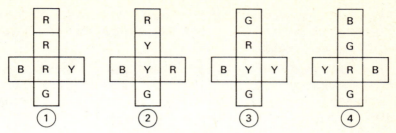

Fig. 3.2   The four cubes

are unable to see all the sides at the same time and we cannot view the entire cube structure all at the same time.

In fact, we could show a cube here by means of three pairs of opposite sides together for, in the problem we are dealing with, the three pairs of opposite sides are independent. Likewise, cube 1 could be represented by the three sets of pairs (RR, RG, BY), that is to say by the graph in Fig. 3.3. In this graph the tips correspond to the colours and the edges to the pairs of colours.

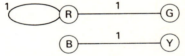

Fig. 3.3   Graph of cube 1

Here we get a global representation of the problem by placing the four graphs which correspond to the four cubes on top of each other.

The problem now remains for us to produce two-part diagrams, each with four independently labelled edges within a diagram. In the graph of Fig. 3.4 we nearly have the answer, and the only solution is found in Fig. 3.5.

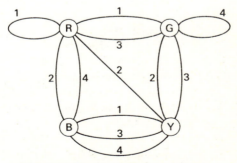

Fig. 3.4   Graph of the four colours

The advantage of illustrating the problem by means of a diagram is obvious. When the structure of the problem is visualized the inevitable result is that the size of the problem is minimized.

Note 4: Right from the start, in the case of Examples 5 and 6, we have extracted the necessary information for solving the problem in hand. For this a diagram which only represents this type of information has to be worked out. Other than synthetic information, the characteristic of a good diagram is the smallness of the amount of information it contains.

Note 5: Examples 3, 4, 5, and 6 show the usefulness of what is known as 'separating the representation of information and its demonstration'.

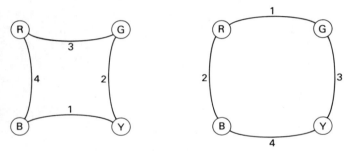

Fig. 3.5 Solution

Likewise, in each of the four examples, the representation of information, which corresponds to a translation of bare facts, is immediate once the form of diagrammatic representation has been chosen. Therefore, from this representation, the demonstration is very simple. The usual cause of difficulty in the solution of these problems is that we tend to carry out the two operations simultaneously; i.e., the interpretation of the text at the same time as its demonstration. This really does bring to mind the popular old saying that a problem which is well posed is already half solved.

It certainly appears to be the case that what is called 'abstraction' means the possibility of having an inner representation of the useful data for a problem thus being able to reason more easily about this than about reality.

Finally, when you look at the representation of information, the fundamental problem lies in the reasoning behind the choice of its representation. Example 6 (instant insanity) gives a good demonstration of the fact that however good the diagram is that you choose it may be that the diagram is not always clear.

3.3 Metaknowledge

We, in fact, do not reason in the same way as an expert system such as referred to in Chapter 2. We use strategic rules in order to avoid the exhaustive numbering of all the facts which may be broken down. In order to do this we must first of all work out a plan for demonstration.

The notorious 'son of Ariane' spoken about by the philosopher and mathematician G. W. Leibnitz (1646–1716) said: 'La véritable méthode nous doit fournir un filum Ariadnes, c'est-à-dire un certain moyen sensible et grossier, qui conduise l'esprit comme sont les lignes tracées en géométrie et les formes des opérations qu'on prescrit aux apprentis en Arithmétique. Sans cela notre esprit ne saurait faire un long chemin sans s'égarer.' This translates to mean, 'True method should provide us with an Ariadne string, which is to say a sensitive and crude way, which leads the mind as do the lines used in geometry and the methods given to students of mathematics. Without this our minds would not know how to follow a long path without getting lost.'

This knowledge about the way in which information should be used is known as 'metaknowledge'. In those expert systems which are based on the rules of production this metaknowledge is shown in the rules which are known as 'metarules'.

In MYCIN (Shortliffe, 1976), a system designed to help medical decisions, the following metarules are found.

Metarule 1

IF you are looking for a cure,
THEN, in this order, consider the rules which allow you to:

1. Obtain clinical information on the patient.
2. Find out which organisms, if any, are the cause of the infection.
3. Identify the organisms which are most like them.
4. Find all the most potentially useful drugs.
5. Choose the suitable drugs for use in small quantities.

Metarule 2

IF 1. The patient is at risk,
   2. Any rules exist which mention pseudo-monies in a premise,
   3. Any rules exist which mention klebsiellas in a premise,
THEN it is likely that he would fail to use the first ones before the second.

Metarule 3

IF 1. The location of the growth bacteria is not sterile,
   2. Any rules exist which mention in their premises an organism which has

already occurred in this particular patient and which could in fact be the same as the one you are looking for,
THEN it is certain that neither of the rules may be used.

Metarule 1 gives the general plan for finding a cure.
Metarule 2 proposes using certain rules in preference to others.
Metarule 3 proposes excluding certain rules. One very important point is that metarules call up rules according to their content and not their names, Indeed, in this case, they allow the system to adapt itself to any additions, rejections, or modifications of the rules without the necessity of any new programming. The performance of a system will therefore depend strongly on the qualities of the metarules which are to be introduced. And these are the most difficult to determine!

In order to elaborate on the strategies and plans the system must have metarules available which, most importantly, allow it to:

— know what is known,
— 'Know what you know you know and know what you don't know', as Confucius so rightly said,
— decide what importance to give the information,
— organize the knowledge base and create new concepts,
— alter the representation (as in ALICE where two types of representation are used simultaneously).

It is by introducing metarules which answer these questions that most progress is likely to be made with expert systems; cf., for example, MECHO (Bundy *et al.*, 1979), CRYSALIS (Engelmore and Terry, 1979), and AM (Lenat, 1977).

4. Representation of information in SNARK

In this chapter we summarize the representation of information used in the SNARK system devised by J. L. Laurière (1982c) and also in ALOUETTE devised by Mulet-Marquis (1983).

4.1 Facts in SNARK

Let us consider the following sentence:

'Jean gives a book to Paul.'

There is a compound relationship between Jean, the giver, Paul, the recipient, and book, the gift. It is a relationship with three attributes: giver, gift, and recipient. In the language of the relational database the relationship corresponds to the R relationship (Giver, Gift, Recipient), the instantiation of which in this case would be (Jean, book, Paul). (*Translator's note*: 'instantiation' is the process of allocating specific values to attributes stored in a knowledge base.)

We do not need the finished article 'Jean gives the book to Paul' in the various uses we will have to make of the fact: we only have to use 'Jean gives something to Paul', 'Someone gives the book to Paul', 'Jean gives the book to someone', 'Jean gives something to someone', etc.

As a result it is most important to break down the original facts into modules. On the other hand, it would, of course, be really useful to have a standard representation of basic facts so that they could be manipulated very easily.

The choice which SNARK adopts is to represent all the facts by binary relationships thanks to an intermediary floating variable (*Translator's note*: called a 'zombie' in the original) which is an entity which does not exactly exist in itself, but is defined according to its relationship with others. With the fact 'Jean gives the book to Paul' we associate the floating variable indicated by $a where the number, or label, of the floating variable $a and the three binary relationships are:

Gift ($a) = book
Giver ($a) = Jean
Recipient ($a) = Paul

More precisely, a fact will be represented by a triplet of the form:

OBJECT, ATTRIBUTE, VALUE, coeff

where:

- ATTRIBUTE corresponds to a binary relationship either to a unique value (e.g., NAME, AGE, FATHER) which we will call a FUNCTION, or to multiple values (e.g., SON, ELEMENT) which we call a RELATION.
- VALUE corresponds either to a constant numeric, or alphabetic, or to an OBJECT.
- coeff is a coefficient of probability which is between 0 and 1.

In order to simplify this the coefficient is omitted in the following examples, where it is always equal to 1. Thus 'Jean gives the book to Paul' can be described by SNARK in the following way:

$001, Giver, Jean
$001, Recipient, Paul
$001, Gift Book

Facts such as 'The tyre is an element of the wheel' and 'the wheel is an element of the bicycle' may be described in SNARK by:

$004, Nature, tyre
$002, Nature, wheel
$003, Nature, bicycle
$002, Element, $004
$003, Element, $002

where the last fact is interpreted as '$002 is an element of $003'. Finally, 'Babies are illogical' and 'Alan does not look for arnica and rhododendron' may be described respectively by SNARK as:

$005, Nature, Babies
$005, Logical, No

and

$006, Name, Alan
$006, ⌐ collects, Arnica
$006, ⌐ collects, Rhododendron

All the above facts are allocated a coefficient of probability of 1, but we could write the last relationship as:

$006, collects, Rhododendron, 0

You will notice that a R b is interpreted as R(a) = b, or b is R(a).

4.2 Rules in SNARK

These are the 'production rules' which have the following form:

Rule 1

IF ⟨condition⟩
. . . .
  ⟨condition⟩
THEN ⟨action⟩ coeff
      . . . . . .
          ⟨action⟩ coeff
End of Rule

where ⟨condition⟩ and ⟨action⟩ are combined to produce an expression of the form:

ATTRIBUTE (x) ⟨operator⟩ ⟨value⟩

and where

− x is a variable name which is instantiated by the floating variables in the base of facts.
− ⟨operator⟩ is a symbol such as =, ⟩=, ⟨=, ⟨, ⟩ to which the symbols ⟸ and ← are added for ⟨action⟩.
− ⟨value⟩ is either a numeric constant, an alphanumeric, or an expression.

The double arrow ⟸ is analogous to the assignment operator in programming languages. The value part is assigned to ATTRIBUTE (x) with the erasure of the old value.

The single arrow ← signifies that ⟨value⟩ is simply added to the whole group of values of ATTRIBUTE (x) without erasure.

In addition, the action

CREATE ⟨expression⟩

allows a new object to be introduced into the base of facts, the expression being replaced by a free floating variable index from the outset of the rule. Other actions which correspond to the extensions of language are possible without altering the basic structure.

The four rules in Example 3 are easily described in SNARK:

Rule 2

IF Come within arm's length of a crocodile (x) = yes
THEN Despised (y) = no

Rule 2a

IF Despised (y) = yes
THEN Come within arm's length of a crocodile (y) = no

The transitivity of the relationship of belonging is written down thus:

IF Element (y) = x
   Element (z) = y
THEN Element (z) = x

4.3   An example of helping a diagnosis

Here we will put forward a micro expert system which is linked to a problem of diagnosis.

The knowledge base in SNARK is only the translation of the organigram of the diagnosis 5 mm after the safety injection into the central PWR 900 MW.

Knowledge base

Rule 1

IF Pprim(t) > 138
   Pprim(t) < 160
   $\wedge$ PGV(t) < 4
Purges GV or condenser (t) = non-activated
THEN Diagnosis(t) $\leftarrow$ is excessive
     Procedure(t) $\leftarrow 13$

Rule 2

IF Pprimt(t) $< = 138$
THEN Diagnosis(t) $\leftarrow$ breach

Rule 3

IF Prim(t) > = 160
THEN Diagnosis(t) ← breach

Rule 4

IF ∧ PGV(t) > = 4
THEN Diagnosis(t) ← breach

Rule 5

IF Purges GV or condenser(t) = activated
THEN Diagnosis(t) ← Rupture of GV tube
        Procedure(t) ← A3

Rule 6

IF Diagnosis(t) = breach
    Purges GV or condenser(t) = non-activated
THEN Diagnosis(t) ← breach primary or secondary

Rule 7

IF Diagnosis(t) = Breach primary or secondary
∧ PGV(t) > = 20
THEN Diagnosis(t) ← Breach secondary

Rule 8

IF Diagnosis(t) = breach primary or secondary
    ∧ PGV(t) < 20
    PGVmax(t) > = Pprim(t) + 10
THEN Diagnosis(t) ← APRP (large breach)
        Procedure(t) ← A12

Rule 9

IF Diagnosis(t) = primary or secondary breach
    PGVmax(t) < Pprim(t) + 10
    PGVmax(t) < 40
THEN Diagnosis(t) ← secondary breach

Rule 10

IF Diagnosis(t) = primary or secondary breach
    ∧ PGV(t) < 20
    PGVmax(t) < Pprim(t) + 10
    PGVmax(t) > = 40
THEN Diagnosis(t) ← primary breach

Rule 11

IF Diagnosis(t) = secondary breach
   Tric(t) > = 286
THEN Diagnosis(t) ← secondary breach surrounded (overheating)
      Procedure ← A23

Rule 12

IF Diagnosis(t) = secondary breach
   Tric(t) > = 286
   P surrounded(t) = abnormally raised
THEN Diagnosis(t) ← secondary breach surrounded (cooling)
      Procedure(t) ← A22

Rule 13

IF Diagnosis(t) = secondary breach
   Tric(t) < 286
   P surrounded(t) = normal
THEN Diagnosis(t) ← Rupture of steam tube outside surrounded area
      Procedure(t) ← A21

Rule 14

IF Diagnosis(t) = primary breach
   Vanne Dech pressure or asp norm(t) = wide open
THEN Diagnosis(t) ← Press rap primary Circuit by pressure
      Procedure(t) ← AB

Rule 15

IF Diagnosis(t) = primary breach
   Vanne Dech Pressure or asp norm(t) = not wide open
   Pprim(t) > PGVmax(t)
THEN Diagnosis(t) ← APRP (small breach)
      Procedure(t) ← A11

Rule 16

IF Diagnosis(t) = primary breach
   Vanne Dech pressure or Asp norm(t) = not wide open
   Pprim(t) < = PGV max(t)
THEN Diagnosis(t) ← APRP (large breach)
      Procedure(t) ← A12

Initial base of facts

Currently, the base of facts is made up of the values of various parameters and several coefficients taken from these values. For example:

Pprimt(t) = 72
Tric(t) = 287
PGVmax(t) = 71
PGVmin(t) = 70
$\wedge$ PGV(t) = 1
($\wedge$ PGV = PGVmax $-$ PGVmin)
Purged GV or Condenser(t) = not activated
Psurrounded(t) = 2
Vanne Dech pressure or Asp Norm(t) = not wide open

Starting from this initial base of facts we can trigger off all the rules for which the premises have been satisfied. The order in which the rules should be applied is: 2, 6, 10, 15. The last fact shown gives the diagnosis and the necessary procedure to take.

When we question the system it gives rules which were useful for demonstration purposes, so that the complete explanation of the reasoning is:

Starting from the following known facts:

Pprim(t) = 72

By means of Rule 2 we deduce the fact that

Diagnosis(t) = Breach

Starting from the following known facts:

Diagnosis(t) = Breach
Purged GV or condenser(t) = not activated

By means of rule 6 we deduce the fact that

Diagnosis(t) = primary or secondary Breach

Starting from the following known facts:

Diagnosis(t) = primary or secondary Breach
$\wedge$ PGV(t) = 1
PGVmax(t) = 71
Pprim(t) = 72

By means of Rule 10 we deduce the following fact:

Diagnosis(t) = primary breach

Starting from the following facts:

Diagnosis(t) = primary breach
Vanne Dech Pressure or Asp norm(t) = not wide open
Pprim(t) = 72
PGVmax(t) = 71

By means of Rule 15 we deduce the following fact:

Diagnosis(t) = APRP (Small Breach)
Procedure(t) = A11

Certain points can be learned from the above example. They are that:

- The explicit writing of each rule forces an extra reflection on its truth and could lead to improvements. SNARK is therefore a language of specification.
- The improvements are brought about simply by changing one rule for another without touching any of the others.
- SNARK's rules are also the computer program which makes the diagnosis. It is sufficient, then, for the expert to specify his problem without resorting to writing programs. The reliability of the solution to the problem is thus improved.
- Since the introduction of the rules into the program is so straightforward it is therefore natural to introduce even more of them in order to obtain an even more accurate diagnosis.
- The introduction of coefficients of similarity (which did not appear in the above example) could allow us to take account of the compromises which were made when the terms were chosen.

Further work on these points have been made by Gondran, Hery, and Laleuf (1983).

4.4 Simulation of archaeological reasoning

We shall now examine the simulation of reasoning in the field of archaeology. To the best of the author's knowledge this is the first non-trivial example in the field of human sciences. It is the result of studies on the process of archaeological reasoning; see Gardin and Lagrange (1975) and Gardin (1979).

The authoresses, Lagrange and Renaud (1982) formalized and simulated the interpretation of a bas-relief studied by Roux (1971), shown in Fig. 4.1. They then used the SNARK language formally to describe everything which was known about the subject and the base of facts corresponds to the descrip-

Fig. 4.1   The bas-relief used for the interpretation

tion of the bas-relief (61 facts in SNARK) and the base of rules needed for their interpretation (42 rules in SNARK).

Initial base of facts

(External representation by SNARK by replacing a floating variable with a noun; the base corresponds to a description of Fig. 4.1)

1. Facts which describe the origin and outer characteristics of the bas-relief:

PLACE	(RAMPART)	= TOWN-DE-KONYA
ELEMENT	(RAMPART)	= ROCK-FIG
DATE	(RAMPART)	= 1221
LENGTH	(ROCK-FIG)	= 55
WIDTH	(ROCK-FIG)	= 50
NATURE	(ROCK-FIG)	= ROCK-FIG

2. General description of the bas-relief:

ELEMENT	(ROCK-FIG)	= DECOR (ROCK-FIG) = SCENE

ELEMENT	(SCENERY)	= PERSON1, PERSON2, SEAT1,
		BIRD1
MODE	(SCENERY)	= STATIC, SERIOUS
NATURE	(PERSON1)	= NATURE (PERSON2) = PERSON
POSTURE	(PERSON1)	= SITTING
POSTURE	(PERSON2)	= STANDING
APPEARANCE	(BIRD1)	= BIG

3. Detailed description of the bas-relief:

CLOTHING	(R HAND-P1)	= GLOVED
CLOTHING	(L HAND-P1)	= GLOVELESS
ASPECT	(SEAT 1)	= FOLDING SEAT
R-HAND	(PERSON1)	= R-HAND-P1
L-HAND	(PERSON1)	= L-HAND-P1
R-HAND	(PERSON2)	= R-HAND-P2
L-HAND	(PERSON2)	= L-HAND-P2
SASH	(PERSON1)	= SASH-P1
SASH	(PERSON2)	= SASH-P2
NATURE	(BIRD1)	= BIRD
POSITION	(BIRD1)	= V.CLEAR
OPPOSITE	(PERSON1)	= PERSON2
SEAT	(PERSON1)	= SEAT1
DIRECTION	(PERSON2)	= R-HAND-P1
ABOVE	(WAIST-P1)	= WAIST-P2
CONTENTS	(R-HAND-P1)	= BIRD1
CONTENTS	(L-HAND-P1)	= CHIN-P2
CONTENTS	(R-HAND-P2)	= SASH-P1
CONTENTS	(L-HAND-P2)	= SASH-P2
WAIST	(PERSON1)	= WAIST-P1
WAIST	(PERSON2)	= WAIST-P2
CLOTHING	(PERSON1)	= CLOTH-P1
CLOTHING	(PERSON2)	= CLOTH-P2
SAME-CLOTH	(R-HAND-P1)	= R-HAND-P1

Knowledge base

RULE NUMBER: SL01
RULE
IF CENTURY $\qquad$ (S) = 13

```
IF COUNTRY            (S) = ANATOLIA
IF ELEMENT            (S) = (P)
IF NATURE             (P) = PERSON
THEN
   NATION             (P) ⇐ WEST TURKEY
   PERIOD             (S) ← SELDJOUK
FR
RULE NUMBER: SL02
RULE
IF NATURE             (D) = SCENE
IF CONTENTS           (D) = TRAD-CYN
IF ELEMENT            (D) = (P)
IF NATION             (P) = WEST TURKEY
IF PERIOD             (D) = SELDJOUK
THEN
   CONTENTS           (D) ← TRAD-CYN-TURK-GOLD
FR
RULE NUMBER: SL03
RULE
IF NATURE             (S) = SCENE
IF ELEMENT            (S) = (X)
IF ELEMENT            (S) = (Y)
IF NATURE             (X) = PERSON
IF NATURE             (Y) = PERSON
IF R-HAND             (X) = (M)
IF SASH               (X) = (C)
IF CONTENTS           (M) = (C)
IF PERIOD             (S) = SELDJOUK
THEN
   DEMONSTRATION      (X) ⇐ OBEDIENCE
FR
RULE NUMBER: SL04
RULE
IF NATURE             (E) = SCENE
IF BELONGS            (E) = ICON-SELDJOUK
IF ELEMENT            (E) = (P)
IF NATURE             (P) = PERSON
IF R-HAND             (P) = (M)
IF CONTENTS           (M) = (O)
IF ELEMENT            (E) = (O)
IF NATURE             (O) = BIRD
```

```
IF POSITION              (O) = V. CLEAR
THEN
   FUNCTION              (P) ⇐ FALCONER
   IDENTITY              (O) ⇐ FALCON
FR
RULE NUMBER: SL05
RULE
IF NATURE                (E) = SCENE
IF CONTENTS              (E) = TRAD-CYN-TURK-GOLD
IF ELEMENT               (E) = (P)
IF NATURE                (P) = PERSON
IF AGE                   (P) = CHILD-ADOLESC
IF STATUS                (P) = HIGH RANK
THEN
   ROLE                  (P) ⇐ REC-INVEST-HUNT
FR
RULE NUMBER: SL06
RULE
IF NATURE                (E) = SCENE
IF CONTENTS              (E) = TRAD-CYN-TURK-GOLD
IF ELEMENT               (E) = (P)
IF NATURE                (P) = PERSON
IF PLACE                 (P) = OPEN AIR
IF ACTION                (P) = SPECTATOR
IF STATUS                (P) = IMPORTANT
THEN
   RANK                  (P) ⇐ DIGNITARY
FR
RULE NUMBER: SL07
RULE
IF PERIOD                (S) = SELDJOUK
IF ELEMENT               (S) = (O)
IF IDENT                 (O) = FALCON
IF ELEMENT               (S) = (M)
IF R-HAND                (P) = (M)
IF CONTENTS              (M) = (O)
IF RANK                  (P) = DIGNITARY
THEN
   SIGNIF                (O) ⇐ SYMBOL-IMPERIAL
   IDENT                 (P) ⇐ SULTAN
FR
RULE NUMBER: SL08
```

```
RULE
IF PERIOD              (S) = SELDJOUK
IF ELEMENT             (S) = (P)
IF STATUS              (P) = IMPORTANT
THEN
   RANK                (P) ⇐ DIGNITARY
FR
RULE NUMBER: SL09
RULE
IF PERIOD              (E) = SELDJOUK
IF NATURE              (E) = CEREM-HUNT
IF ELEMENT             (E) = (P)
IF NATION              (P) = WEST TURKEY
IF IDENT               (P) = SULTAN
THEN
   DESCRIPTION         (E) ⇐ PRAC-RIT-HUNT
   PREROGATIVE         (P) ← RIGHT-HUNT
FR
RULE NUMBER: SU10
RULE
IF DATE                (R) = 1299
IF DATE                (R) = 1200
THEN
   CENTURY             (R) ⇐ 13
FR
RULE NUMBER: SU11
RULE
IF PLACE               (R) = TOWN-DE-KONYA
THEN
   COUNTRY             (R) ⇐ ANATOLIA
FR
RULE NUMBER: SU12
RULE
IF NATURE              (R) = RAMPART
IF ELEMENT             (R) = (F)
IF NATURE              (F)STONE-FIG
THEN
   SITUATION           (F) ⇐ REUSE
FR
RULE NUMBER: SU13
RULE
IF SITUATION           (Y) = REUSE
```

```
IF ELEMENT            (X) = (Y)
IF CENTURY            (X) = (Z)
THEN
   CENTURY            (Y) ⇐ (Z)
FR
RULE NUMBER: SU14
RULE
IF CENTURY            (X) = (Z)
IF COUNTRY            (X) = (A)
IF ELEMENT            (X) = (Y)
THEN
   CENTURY            (Y) ⇐ (Z)
   COUNTRY            (Y) ⇐ (A)
FR
RULE NUMBER: SU15
RULE
IF NATURE             (P) = STONE-FIG
IF WIDTH              (P) > = 50
IF LENGTH             (P) > 55
IF DECOR              (P) = (S)
IF NATURE             (S) = SCENE
THEN
   IDENT              (P) ⇐ FUNEREAL STELE
FR
RULE NUMBER: SU16
RULE
IF BIGGER             (X) = (Y)
IF WAIST              (A) = (X)
IF NATURE             (A) = PERSON
IF WAIST              (B) = (Y)
IF NATURE             (B) = PERSON
THEN
   STATUS             (A) ← SUPERIOR
FR
RULE NUMBER: SU17
RULE
IF BIGGER             (X) = (Y)
IF WAIST              (A) = (X)
IF NATURE             (A) = PERSON
IF WAIST              (B) = (Y)
IF NATURE             (B) = PERSON
```

```
IF AGE                 (A) = ADULT
THEN
   AGE                 (B) ⇐ CHILD-ADOLESC
FR
RULE NUMBER: SU18
RULE
IF CLOTHING            (X) = (A)
IF CLOTHING            (Y) = (B)
IF NATURE              (X) = PERSON
IF NATURE              (Y) = PERSON
IF NATURE              (A) = NATURE (B)
THEN
   SAME-LINE           (X) ← (Y)
FR
RULE NUMBER: SU19
RULE
IF NATURE              (X) = PERSON
IF POSTURE             (X) = SITTING
IF NATURE              (Y) = PERSON
IF POSTURE             (Y) = STANDING
THEN
   STATUS              (X) ← SUPERIOR
FR
RULE NUMBER: SU20
RULE
IF IDENTITY            (X) = FUNEREAL STELE
IF DECOR               (X) = (S)
IF NATURE              (S) = SCENE
THEN
   CREATE              (P)
   ELEMENT             (S) ← (P)
   STATUS              (P) ← IMPORTANT
   NATURE              (P) ← PERSON
FR
RULE NUMBER: SU21
RULE
IF NATURE              (P) = PERSON
IF CONTENTS            (D) = (O)
IF R-HAND              (P) = (D)
IF NATURE              (O) = BIRD
IF ASPECT              (O) = BIG
```

```
IF L-HAND              (P) = (G)
IF CLOTHING            (G) = GLOVELESS
IF CLOTHING            (D) = GLOVED
THEN
  IDENT                (O) ⇐ FALCON
FR
RULE NUMBER: SU22
RULE
IF NATURE              (S) = SCENE
IF MODE                (S) = STATIC
IF MODE                (S) = SERIOUS
THEN
  SIGNIF               (S) ⇐ CEREMONY
FR
RULE NUMBER: SU23
RULE
R-HAND                 (X) = (M)
IF DIRECTION           (M) = (Y)
IF NATURE              (X) = PERSON
IF NATURE              (Y) = PERSON
IF CONTENTS            (M) = (Z)
THEN
  QUALITY              (Z) ⇐ GIFT
  SITUATION            (X) ⇐ GIVER
  SITUATION            (Y) ⇐ RECIPIENT
FR
RULE NUMBER: SU24
RULE
IF DECOR               (P) = (S)
IF NATURE              (S) = SCENE
IF ELEMENT             (S) = (O)
IF IDENT               (O) = FALCON
THEN
  NAT-OF-S             (S) ← HUNTING
FR
RULE NUMBER: SU25
RULE
IF SIGNIF              (S) = CEREMONY
IF NAT-OF-S            (S) = HUNTING
THEN
  NATURE               (S) ← CEREM-HUNTING
FR
```

RULE NUMBER: SU26
RULE
IF SAME LINE   (X) = (Y)
IF NATURE   (X) = PERSON
IF NATURE   (Y) = PERSON
IF AGE   (X) = ADULT
IF AGE   (Y) = CHILD-ADOLESC
THEN
   SON   (X) ← (Y)
   FATHER   (Y) ← (X)
FR
RULE NUMBER: SU27
RULE
IF IDEN   (P) = SULTAN
THEN
   AGE   (P) ⇐ ADULT
FR
RULE NUMBER: SU28
RULE
IF ASPECT   (S) = FOLDING SEAT
THEN
   FUNCTION   (S) ⇐ OPEN-AIR-SEAT
FR
RULE NUMBER: SU29
RULE
IF POSTURE   (P) = SITTING
IF SEAT   (P) = (A)
IF FUNCTION   (A) = OPEN-AIR-SEAT
THEN
   FUNCTION   (P) ⇐ OPEN-AIR
FR
RULE NUMBER: SU30
RULE
IF NATURE   (S) = SCENE
IF PEROOD   (S) = SELDJOUK
THEN
   BELONGS   (S) ⇐ ICON-SELDJOUK
FR
RULE NUMBER: SU31
RULE
IF SON   (X) = (Y)
IF IDENT   (X) = SULTAN

```
THEN
   IDENT                  (Y) ⇐ SON-SULTAN
   STATUT                 (Y) ← HIGH-RANK
FR
RULE NUMBER: SU32
RULE
IF NATURE                 (S) = SCENE
IF NATURE                 (S) = CEREM-HUNTING
THEN
   CONTENTS               (S) ⇐ TRAD-CYN
FR
RULE NUMBER: SU33
RULE
IF NATURE                 (S) = SCENE
IF SIGNIFIC               (S) = CEREMONY
IF ELEMENT                (S) = (X)
IF ELEMENT                (S) = (Y)
IF SITUATION              (X) = GIVER
IF SITUATION              (Y) = RECIPIENT
IF R-HAND                 (X) = (M)
IF CONTENTS               (M) = (D)
IF QUALITY                (D) = GIFT
IF IDENT                  (D) = FALCON
THEN
   SENSE                  (D) ⇐ SYMBOL-RIGHT-HUNT
FR
RULE NUMBER: SU34
RULE
IF NATURE                 (S) = SCENE
IF SIGNIFIC               (S) = CEREMONY
IF ELEMENT                (S) = (X)
IF ELEMENT                (S) = (Y)
IF SITUATION              (X) = GIVER
IF SITUATION              (Y) = RECIPIENT
IF R-HAND                 (X) = (M)
IF CONTENTS               (M) = (D)
IF GRADE                  (Y) = NEOPHYTE
IF SENS                   (D) = SYMBOL-RIGHT-HUNT
THEN
   IDENT                  (S) ⇐ INVESTIT-HUNT
FR
```

RULE NUMBER: SU35
RULE
IF SENSE   (X) = SYMBOL-RIGHT-HUNT
THEN
  CLASSE   (X) ⇐ SYMBOL
FR
RULE NUMBER: SU36
RULE
IF NATURE   (S) = SCENE
IF SIGNIFIC   (S) = CEREMONY
IF ELEMENT   (S) = (X)
IF SITUATION   (X) = RECIPIENT
IF ELEMENT   (S) = (Y)
IF SITUATION   (Y) = GIVER
IF R-HAND   (Y) = (M)
IF CONTENTS   (M) = (D)
IF QUALITY   (D) = GIFT
IF CLASS   (D) = SYMBOL
IF AGE   (X) = CHILD-ADOLESC
IF DEMONSTRATION   (X) = OBEDIENCE
THEN
  GRADE   (X) ⇐ NEOPHYTE
FR
RULE NUMBER: SU37
RULE
IF NATURE   (S) = SCENE
IF DESCRIPTION   (S) = PRAC-RIT-HUNT
IF ELEMENT   (S) = (P)
IF GRADE   (P) = NEOPHYTE
THEN
  IDENT   (S) ⇐ INVESTIT-HUNT
FR
RULE NUMBER: SU38
RULE
IF IDENT   (X) = SULTAN
IF IDENT   (X) = SON-SULTAN
IF AGE   (Y) = CHILD-ADOLESC
THEN
  QUALITY   (Y) ⇐ HEIR-PREROGATIVE
FR
RULE NUMBER: SU39

```
RULE
IF NAT-OF-S          (S) = HUNT
IF ELEMENT           (S) = (P)
IF POSTURE           (P) = SITTING
THEN
   ACTION            (P) ⇐ SPECTATOR
FR
RULE NUMBER: SU40
RULE
IF PERIOD            (S) = SELDJOUK
IF SIGNIFIC          (S) = CEREMONY
IF NATURE            (S) = SCENE
IF ELEMENT           (S) = (P)
IF FUNCTION          (P) = FALCONER
THEN
   NATURE            (S) ← CEREM-HUNT
FR
RULE NUMBER: SU41
RULE
IF NATURE            (S) = SCENE
IF ELEMENT           (S) = (X)
IF SITUATION         (X) = GIVER
IF PREROGATIVE       (X) = RIGHT-HUNT
IF ELEMENT           (S) = (Y)
IF SITUATION         (Y) = RECIPIENT
IF QUALITY           (Y) = HEIR-PREROGATIVE
THEN
   GESTURE           (X) = CONFERRED
   OBJECT-CONFERRED  (X) ⇐ RIGHT-HUNT
FR
RULE NUMBER: SU42
RULE
IF ELEMENT           (S) = (X)
IF NATURE            (X) = PERSON
IF STATUS            (X) = IMPORTANT
IF ELEMENT           (S) = (Y)
IF NATURE            (Y) = PERSON
IF STATUS            (Y) = SUPERIOR
THEN
   KILL              (X)
   STATUS            (Y) ← IMPORTANT
FR
```

If we start from this initial base of facts we may trigger off all the rules for which the premises have been satisfied. From these we may deduce 32 new facts which may be added to the initial base.

The order in which the rules may be applied is as follows: 10, 11, 22, 28, 12, 19, 29, 16, 18, 21, 24, 25, 32, 14 six times, 1 twice, 4 twice, 2 twice, 13, 3.

SNARK did not have to use rules 5, 6, 7, 8, 9, 15, 17, 20, 23, 26, 27, 31, 33, 34, 35, 36, 37, 38, 40, 41, and the last fact demonstrated is

DEMONSTRATION (PERSON2) = OBEDIENCE

On further examination the system gives out rules which have been used for demonstration. Take the case of the last fact discovered using rules 1, 3, 10, 11, and 14. The total examination of the reasoning is:

Starting from the following known facts:

PLACE   (RAMPART) = TOWN-DE KONYA

By using rule 11 we deduce the fact:

COUNTRY   (RAMPART) = ANATOLIA

Starting from the following known facts:

DATE   (RAMPART) = 1221

By means of rule 10 we deduce the following fact:

CENTURY   (RAMPART) = 13

Starting from the following known facts:

CENTURY   (RAMPART) = 13
COUNTRY   (RAMPART) = ANATOLIA
ELEMENT   (RAMPART) = STONE-FIG

By means of rule 14, we deduce the following facts:

CENTURY   (STONE-FIG) = 13
COUNTRY   (STONE-FIG) = ANATOLIA

From the following known facts:

CENTURY   (STONE-FIG) = 13
COUNTRY   (STONE-FIG) = ANATOLIA
ELEMENT   (STONE-FIG) = SCENE

By means of rule 14 we deduce the facts:

CENTURY   (SCENE) = 13
COUNTRY   (SCENE) = ANATOLIA

From the following known facts:

CENTURY	(SCENE) = 13
COUNTRY	(SCENE) = ANATOLIA
ELEMENT	(SCENE) = PERSON1
NATURE	(PERSON1) = PERSON

By means of rule 1 we deduce the fact:

PERIOD   (SCENE) = SELDJOUK

From the following known facts:

NAME	(SCENE) = SCENE
ELEMENT	(SCENE) = PERSON1
ELEMENT	(SCENE) = PERSON2
NATURE	(PERSON2) = PERSON
NATURE	(PERSON1) = PERSON
R-HAND	(PERSON2) = R-HAND-P2
SASH	(PERSON1) = SASH-P1
CONTENTS	(R-HAND-P2) = SASH-P1
PERIOD	(SCENE) = SELDJOUK

By means of rule 3 we deduce the fact:

DEMONSTRATION (PERSON2) = OBEDIENCE

4.5 An example in automatic demonstration (Laurière, 1982c)

In this section we put forward a simple example which shows on the one hand the involvement of first order logic and on the other hand the way in which certain quantifiers may be integrated into the knowledge base.

Knowledge base

Rule 1

IF App (x) = (A)	IF x belongs to A and A included in B
Include (A) = (B)	
THEN App $(x) \leftarrow$ (B)	THEN x belongs to B

Rule 2

IF Elmt (A) = (x)	IF x is a particular element of A and if x
App (x) = (B)	belongs to B
THEN Include (A) $\leftarrow$ (B)	THEN A is included in B

Rule 3

IF Not empty (A) = yes   IF A is not empty
THEN Create (x)   THEN one can create an element x which is
    Elmt (A) ← (x)   an element of A

Rule 4

IF Elmt (A) = (x)   IF x is a particular element of A
THEN App (x) ← (A)   THEN x belongs to A

Initial base of facts (in an external representation of SNARK)

Include $(A_0) = B_0$ i.e., $A_0 \subset B_0$
Include $(B_0) = C_0$ $B_0 \subset C_0$
not empty (A_0) = yes A_0 not empty

If we start from the initial base of facts we trigger off all the rules for which the premises have been satisfied. The order in which the rules are applied is as follows: 3, 4, 1, 1, 2.

The last fact shown is: Include $(A_0) = C_0$, i.e., $A_0 \subset C_0$. So we have shown the theorem of the transitivity of the relationship of inclusion.

On further examination the system will give out rules which were used for demonstration:

From the following known facts:

    not empty (A_0) = YES

By means of Rule 3 we create the floating variable $101 and deduce the fact that

    Elmt (A_0) = $101

By means of Rule 4 we deduce the fact that

    App ($101) = A_0

From the following known facts:

    App ($101) = A_0
    Included $(A_0) = B_0$

By means of Rule 1 we deduce the fact that

    App ($101) = B_0

From the following known facts:

    App ($101) = B_0
    Included $(B_0) = C_0$

By means of Rule 1 we deduce the fact that

App ($101) = C_0

From the following known facts:

Elmt (A_0) = $101
App ($101) = C_0

By means of Rule 2 we deduce the fact that

Include (A_0) = C_0

There are two things to note from this example:

– The quantifier 'whatever' could easily be represented in SNARK if it is dealing with a defined whole 'as an attribute' and not 'as an extension of'. Likewise, the expression

$\forall x \in A$

is simply represented in SNARK by the fact

Elmt (A) = x

– The action CREATE (x) allows us to introduce new elements into the initial base of facts. This is an important point which should check the validity of all expert systems.

We should notice that a wide variety of actions may be slotted into the action part of the rules very easily, especially when it calls for a subprogram.

4.6 An example of problem solving

Here we show how a very simple expert system is allowed to simulate our reasoning in the 'Choose your flower' problem in Chapter 2.

Knowledge base

Rule 1

IF Noncollect (i) = (j)
   Uncollect (i) = (j)
THEN kill fact Uncollect (i) = (j)
      Card Uncollect (i) $\Leftarrow$ Card Uncollect (i) $-$ 1

Rule 2

IF Card Uncollect (i) = 1
   Uncollect (i) = (k)
THEN Collect (i) $\Leftarrow$ (k)

Rule 3

IF Collect (i) = (j)

   Nature (k) = boy

THEN Noncollect (k) $\Leftarrow$ (j)

We have to define a function called 'Collect' and two relationships 'Noncollect' and 'Uncollect' where, for example,

Uncollect (Alan)

corresponds to the whole group of flowers that Alan is able to pick.

Rule 1 keeps the Uncollect groups (i) while taking account of the information about the Noncollect types (i) = j.

Rule 2 shows when an Uncollect (i) group has a cardinal equal to 1; we notice the subjectivity of the 'Collect' function.

Rule 3 allows us to consider the injectivity of the 'Collect' function.

The base of facts looks rather clumsy in SNARK, but it can be constructed automatically.

Base of facts

Uncollect (Alan) = Uncollect (Eric) = Uncollect (Patrick) = Uncollect (Daniel) = Uncollect (John) = Gentian, Arnica, Rhododendron, Edelweiss, Blue Thistle

Card Uncollect (Alan) = Card Uncollect (Eric) = Card Uncollect (Patrick) = Card Uncollect (Daniel) = Card Uncollect (John) = 5

Nature (Alan) = Nature (Eric) = Nature (Patrick) = Nature (Daniel) = Nature (John) = Boy

Noncollect (Alan) = Arnica, Rhododendron, Blue Thistle

Noncollect (John) = Edelweiss, Rhododendron, Blue Thistle

Noncollect (Eric) = Edelweiss

Noncollect (Daniel) = Edelweiss, Blue Thistle

If we begin with these facts we trigger off all the rules for which the premises have been satisfied. The order in which the rules are applied is as follows: 1 ten times, 2 and 3 four times, 1 four times, 2 and 3 three times, 1 three times, 2 and 3 twice, 1 twice, 2, 3, 1, 2.

Rule 1 is first used to reduce the cardinals of the groups Uncollect (i) into 1, 4, 5, 3, and 2 respectively.

Rule 2 is triggered off with

Card Uncollect (Alan) = 1

which leads to

Collect (Alan) = Gentian

This result triggers off Rule 3 which gives

Noncollect (Eric) = Noncollect (Patrick) = Noncollect (Daniel) = Noncollect (John) = Gentian

Rule 1 ends up by reducing the cardinal of Uncollect (i) down to unity. Rule 2 can then end up with

Card Uncollect (John) = 1

which leads to

Collect (John) = Arnica

Rules 3, 1, and 2 are worked out successively in order to give firstly

Collect (Daniel) = Rhododendron

then

Collect (Eric) = Blue Thistle

and thirdly

Collect (Patrick) = Edelweiss

Notice that in the section on action in Rule 1 the action 'kill fact' corresponds to the elimination of a fact from the knowledge base.

5. Structures of some inference engines

As we have seen in Chapters 2 and 4, there is a difference between systems based on propositional logic and those based on first-order logic. There is also a difference between the strategies, forward and backward chaining, employed. There is also a third important difference which separates those systems where backtracking on the facts is possible and those where it is not.

Generally, the system understands a knowledge base which has been formed into rules and metarules (heuristics) by an inference engine, which we will describe later, and work memories which are made up mainly of a whole group of given and deduced facts.

Figure 5.1 has been taken from Laurière, (1982b) and represents the general schema of an expert system which is based on production rules.

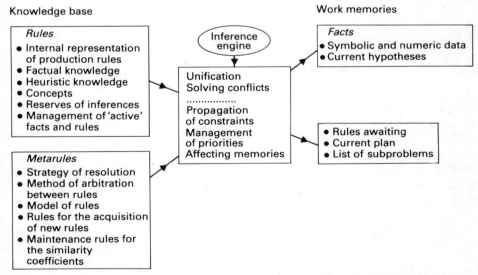

Fig. 5.1 Schema of an expert system based on production rules. (From Laurière, 1982b)

The inference engine, which has complete control of the order of deduction, is the key to the system. A task is always carried out by a sequence of elementary cycles. The true base cycle is shown in Fig. 5.2.

Using first-order logic the Japanese MITI project on fifth-generation computers is aiming to microprogram the three operations shown in Fig. 5.2 so that they are the base operations for machines which deal with knowledge.

Next we present the structure of three inference engines. Two are based on propositional logic and the third is based on first-order logic.

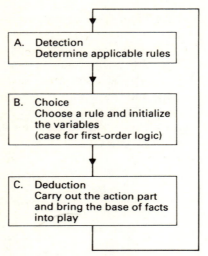

Fig. 5.2   Base cycle of the inference engine

5.1 Inference engines in propositional logic

5.1.1 Forward and backward chaining

There are two reasons why an expert system should be able to make deductions by means of both forward and backward chaining. The first is quite simple. If you begin with a certain number of facts but you do not know the ultimate goal then the forward chain is the most obvious route to take. On the other hand, if you have one or more objectives, or things to check, then backward chaining reduces the number of possible combinations.

The second reason is more complex and calls for a preliminary reflection on the way we think. All our knowledge outside the field of mathematics is based on demonstrative logic, which consists of hypotheses. We are sure about the validity of our mathematical knowledge because of a demonstrative reasoning, whereas we justify our hypotheses by means of plausible reasoning.

To schematize this we could consider that in certain problems we have to deal with two types of knowledge: mechanistic knowledge and some empirical or uncertain knowledge.

Empirical knowledge allows the definition of possible goals and is able to play the role of metaknowledge which we looked at in Chapter 3. This will be used in a forward chain by the inference engine.

Mechanistic knowledge will then be used in backward chaining in order to confirm or reject the goals for which we were aiming.

Finally, backward chaining will have great importance in every case where the system has incomplete information in that particular field. In these cases the expert system should be able to ask for a complete set of pieces of information. Reasoning by means of backward chaining allows for more precision amongst the pieces of information which are the most interesting to obtain.

Most inference engines in the field of propositional logic use the following schema, see for example EMYCIN and SPHINX.

5.1.2 An expert system in LISP

The following expert system has been taken from the excellent book on LISP by Winston and Horn (1981).

The facts for the expert system are written in LISP as:

```
FACTS
    (ANIMAL HAS HAIR)
    (ANIMAL EATS MEAT)
    (ANIMAL HAS TAWNY COLOUR)
    (ANIMAL HAS DARK SPOTS)
```

The rules in this expert system for determining an animal can be represented in LISP in the following ways:

```
(SETQ RULES
    ((RULE IDENTIFY1
            (IF (ANIMAL HAS HAIR))
            (THEN (ANIMAL IS MAMMAL)))
      (RULE IDENTIFY2
            (IF (ANIMAL GIVES MILK))
            (THEN ANIMAL IS MAMMAL)))
      (RULE IDENTIFY3
            (IF (ANIMAL HAS FEATHERS))
            (THEN (ANIMAL IS BIRD)))
```

```
(RULE IDENTIFY4
        (IF (ANIMAL FLIES)
            (ANIMAL LAYS EGGS))
        (THEN (ANIMAL IS BIRD)))
(RULE IDENTIFY5
        (IF (ANIMAL EATS MEAT)
        (THEN (ANIMAL IS CARNIVORE)))
(RULE IDENTIFY6
        (IF (ANIMAL HAS POINTED TEETH)
            (ANIMAL HAS CLAWS)
            (ANIMAL HAS FORWARD EYES))
        (THEN (ANIMAL IS CARNIVORE)))
(RULE IDENTIFY7
        (IF (ANIMAL IS MAMMAL)
            (ANIMAL HAS HOOFS))
        (THEN (ANIMAL IS UNGULATE)))
(RULE IDENTIFY8
        (IF (ANIMAL IS MAMMAL)
            (ANIMAL CHEWS CUD))
        (THEN (ANIMAL IS UNGULATE)
              (EVEN TOED)))
(RULE IDENTIFY9
        (IF (ANIMAL IS MAMMAL)
            (ANIMAL IS CARNIVORE)
            (ANIMAL HAS TAWNY COLOUR)
            (ANIMAL HAS DARK SPOTS))
        (THEN (ANIMAL IS CHEETAH)))
(RULE IDENTIFY10
        (IF (ANIMAL IS MAMMAL)
            (ANIMAL IS CARNIVORE)
            (ANIMAL HAS TAWNY COLOUR)
            (ANIMAL HAS BLACK STRIPES)
        (THEN (ANIMAL IS TIGER)))
(RULE IDENTIFY11
        (IF (ANIMAL IS UNGULATE)
            (ANIMAL HAS LONG NECK)
            (ANIMAL HAS LONG LEGS)
            (ANIMAL HAS DARK SPOTS))
        (THEN (ANIMAL IS GIRAFFE)))
(RULE IDENTIFY12
        (IF (ANIMAL IS UNGULATE)
```

```
            (ANIMAL HAS BLACK STRIPES))
            (THEN (ANIMAL IS ZEBRA)))
   (RULE IDENTIFY13
            (IF (ANIMAL IS BIRD)
            (ANIMAL DOES NOT FLY)
            (ANIMAL HAS LONG NECK)
            (ANIMAL HAS LONG LEGS)
            (ANIMAL IS BLACK AND WHITE))
            (THEN (ANIMAL IS OSTRICH)))
   (RULE IDENTIFY14
            (IF (ANIMAL IS BIRD)
            (ANIMAL DOES NOT FLY)
            (ANIMAL SWIMS)
            (ANIMAL IS BLACK AND WHITE))
   (RULE IDENTIFY15
            (IF (ANIMAL IS BIRD)
            (ANIMAL FLIES WELL))
            (THEN (ANIMAL IS ALBATROSS)))))
```

The keywords RULE, IF, and THEN are only there to help the representation.

Now let us introduce two functions REMEMBER and RECALL in order for us to be able to add new facts to the list of facts and to use them.

REMEMBER adds new facts to FACTS which is used as the free variable.

```
(DEFUN REMEMBER (NEW)
   (COND ((MEMBER NEW FACTS) NIL)
      (T(SETQ FACTS (CONS NEW FACTS))
         (NEW)))
```
If present then do nothing. Otherwise, add and return the added fact.

```
(DEFUN RECALL (FACT)
   (COND ((MEMBER FACT FACTS) FACT)
      (T NIL)))
```
If exists then return it.

From RECALL we can define the function TESTIF which tests whether the premises of a rule have been satisfied.

```
(DEFUN TEST IF(RULE)
      (PROG (IFS)
            (SETQ IFS (CADDR RULE))
            LOOP
```

```
        (COND ((NULL IFS) (RETURN T))      All these facts
              ((RECALL (CAR IFS)))            found?
              (T (RETURN NIL)))             Does the fact
        (SETQ IFS (CDR IFS))                 exist?
        (GO LOOP)))
```

By using REMEMBER and USETHEN you can add new facts for the action section of the rule and in this case SUCCESS is T.

The P function corresponds to a PRINT function.

```
(DEFUN USETHEN (RULE)
        (PROG (THENS SUCCESS)
              (SETQ THENS (CDR (CADDDR RULE)))
              LOOP
              (COND ((NULL THENS) (RETURN SUCCESS))
                    ((REMEMBER (CAR THENS))
                     (P'[Rule] (CADR RULE)
                        '[deduces] (CAR THENS))
                     (SETQ SUCCESS T)))
              (SETQ THENS (CDR THENS))      All these facts added?
              GO LOOP)))                    Add new fact.
```

By adding in TESTIF and USETHEN we define TRYRULE which returns T if and only if the premises are checked and one of the facts from the action section was not already in FACTS.

```
(DEFUN TRYRULE (RULE)
        (AND (TESTIF RULE) (USETHEN RULE)))
```

The forward chaining is thus obtained from the function STEPFORWARD which analyses the list of rules until it has found a usable rule and the function DEDUCE which repeats STEPFORWARD until it is exhausted.

```
(DEFUN STEPFORWARD ( )
        (PROG (RULELIST)
              (SETQ RULELIST RULES)
              LOOP
              (COND ((NULL RULELIST) (RETURN NIL))
                    ((TRYRULE (CAR RULE)) (RETURN T)))
              (SETQ RULELIST (CDR RULELIST))    More rules?
              (GO LOOP)                         Test this rule.

(DEFUN DEDUCE ( )
        (PROG (PROGRESS)
              LOOP
```

```
(COND ((STEPFORWARD) (SETQ PROGRESS T))
      (T (RETURN PROGRESS)))
(GO LOOP)))
```

Thus from the initial facts and the base of rules, the program will use rules 1, 5, and 9 in succession in order to deduce whether the animal is a 'Cheetah'.

Backward chaining is more complex for it calls for the definition of a recursive function VERIFY, which must:

– See if the hypothesis of the aim is in the list of facts.
– If not then draw up the list of rules for which this aim is in the action section.
– If no such rules exist then it must ask for the information to be completed.
– Use TRYRULE to see whether this aim is directly deducable.
– Use TRYRULE + to see whether this aim is indirectly deducable.

The function TRYRULE + is defined with TESTIF + in place of TESTIF. The only difference is that TESTIF + uses VERIFY where TESTIF uses RECALL (from where we get a double recursion).

```
(DEFUN VERIFY (FACT)
      (PROG (RELEVANT1 RELEVANT2)
            (COND ((RECALL FACT) (RETURN T)))
            (SETQ RELEVANT1 (INTHEN FACT))
            (SETQ RELEVANT2 RELEVANT1)
            (COND ((NULL RELEVANT1)
                  (COND ((MEMBER  FACT  ASKED)  (RE-
                  TURN NIL))
                  (AND (P'[is this true:] FACT) (READ))
                  (REMEMBER FACT)
                  (RETURN T))
                  (T (SETQ ASKED (CONS FACT ASKED))
                  (RETURN NIL)))))
      LOOP1
      (COND ((NULL RELEVANT1) GO LOOP2))
      ((TRYRULE (CAR RELEVANT1)) (RETURH T)))
      (SETQ RELEVANT1 (CDR RELEVANT1))
      (GO LOOP1)
      LOOP2
      (COND ((NULL RELEVANT2) (GO EXIT))
      ((TRYRULE + (CAR RELEVANT2)) (RETURN T)))
      (SETQ RELEVANT2 (CDR RELEVANT2))
      (GO LOOP2)
```

```
            EXIT
            (RETURN NIL)))

(DEFUN TESTIF+ (RULE)
        (PROG (IFS)
                (SETQ IFS (CADDR RULE))
                LOOP
                (COND ((NULL IFS) (RETURN T))
                        ((VERIFY (CAR IFS)))
                        (T (RETURN NIL)))
                (SETQ IFS (CDR IFS))
                (GO LOOP)))

(DEFUN TRYRULE+ (RULE)
        (AND (TESTIF+ RULE) (USE THEN RULE)))
```

The function INTHEN checks each rule to see whether the aim is in the action section. It assembles the candidate rules. It uses the predicate THENP for the appropriateness of the fact in a given rule.

```
(DEFUN INTHEN(FACT)
        (MAPCAN '(LAMBDA (R)
                        (COND ((THENP FACT R)
                                LIST R))))
                (RULES))
(DEFUN THENP (FACT RULE)
        (MEMBER FACT (CADDDR RULE)))
```

The variable ASKED is controlled by VERIFY so that VERIFY does not keep asking the same question. ASKED is linked to the function DIAGNOSE which runs the list of hypotheses using VERIFY until one of these hypotheses is confirmed.

```
(DEFUN DIAGNOSE ( )
        (PROG (POSSIBILITIES ASKED)
        (SETQ POSSIBILITIES ASKED)
        LOOP
        (COND ((NULL POSSIBILITIES)
                (P' [No hypotheses can be confirmed.])
                (RETURN NIL))
                (VERIFY (CAR POSSIBILITIES))
                (P' [Hypothesis] (CAR POSSIBILITIES) '[is true.])
                (RETURN (CAR POSSIBILITIES)))))
```

```
            (SETQ POSSIBILITIES (CDR POSSIBILITIES)
            (GO LOOP)))
```

Note that HYPOTHESES is the third free variable after FACTS and RULES.

Let us suppose that HYPOTHESES is defined by:

```
(SETQ HYPOTHESES
       '((ANIMAL IS ALBATROSS)
         (ANIMAL IS PENGUIN)
         (ANIMAL IS OSTRICH)
         (ANIMAL IS ZEBRA)
         (ANIMAL IS GIRAFFE)
         (ANIMAL IS TIGER)
         (ANIMAL IS CHEETAH)))
```

The dialogue generated by the expert system is as follows:

```
(DIAGNOSE)
Is this true: ANIMAL HAS FEATHERS
     NO
Is this true: ANIMAL FLIES
     NO
Is this true: ANIMAL HAS HAIR
     YES
Rule IDENTIFY1 deduces ANIMAL IS MAMMAL
Is this true: ANIMAL HAS HOOFS
     NO
Is this true: ANIMAL CHEWS CUD
     NO
Is this true: ANIMAL EATS MEAT
     YES
Rule IDENTIFY5 deduces ANIMAL IS CARNIVORE
Is this true: ANIMAL HAS TAWNY COLOUR
     YES
Is this true: ANIMAL HAS BLACK STRIPES
     NO
Is this true: ANIMAL HAS DARK SPOTS
     YES
Rule IDENTIFY9 deduces ANIMAL IS CHEETAH
Hypothesis ANIMAL IS CHEETAH is true.
```

By changing the order of the hypotheses and by putting CHEETAH first, the effect from DIAGNOSE will be different and the result would be the following dialogue:

Is this true: ANIMAL HAS HAIR
    YES
Rule IDENTIFY1 deduces ANIMAL IS MAMMAL
Is this true: ANIMAL EATS MEAT
    YES
Rule IDENTIFY5 deduces ANIMAL IS CARNIVORE
Is this true: ANIMAL HAS DARK SPOTS
    YES
Rule IDENTIFY9 deduces ANIMAL IS CHEETAH
Hypothesis ANIMAL IS CHEETAH is true.
(ANIMAL IS CHEETAH)

5.1.3 An inference engine in Pseudo-Algol

Next we come to another approach for constructing an inference engine. The presentation comes from the DEA report of C. Marquant (1982).

The facts of this expert system correspond to a series of key words (for example: poor ignition, irregular ignition) which are able to take one of three values: *true, false,* or *unknown.* A property is assigned to each fact; is it askable or not?

The rules are taken in this way:

IF fact 1 true/false
  and fact 2 true/false

    . . . .

THEN fact N true/false

We notice that here is a rule with just one conclusion. It is put in a disjunctive form which corresponds to the inner representation of the rules. So that the rule:

IF P true and Q false THEN R true gives the logical formula:
'P false or Q true or R true'

This representation is the one chosen by PROLOG, but here we find ourselves in propositional logic while PROLOG works with first-order logic. This representation provides a certain economy of expression. In fact, the preceding logical formula is the equivalent of one of the following three rules:

IF P true and Q false THEN R true
IF P true and R false THEN Q true
IF Q false and R false THEN P false

The use of rules in a disjunctive form clearly defines their nature; it is a question of relationships between the values of the facts, which should be continually checked. In other words, these are the constraints which assure the coherence of the data.

A rule is triggered off as soon as all the elements but one are contradicted; the last one is therefore obliged to be checked. For example, the preceding logical formula will be triggered off if Q and R are false, leading to the fact that P is false.

A rule may be eliminated for two reasons:

1. It has been triggered off. All the facts contained within it have been evaluated. The rule is now eliminated.
2. One of the elements is verified. The others are able to take on certain values. The rule here, too, is eliminated.

The elimination of rules is irreversible. It is only possible in the case of rules which have no variable. In this last case it is getting more and more difficult to affirm that a rule will be no longer of use; see PROLOG.

In order to memorize the state of each rule a value is attached to it which contains the number of indeterminate elements within the rule if it is active and a zero if it has been triggered off or eliminated.

For example, if P is true and Q and R undefined, then the rule 'P false or Q true or R true' has a value of 2. The rule 'P true or Q true' has a value of 0.

Forward chaining is quite simple. Each new fact eliminates all the possible rules. The value of the rules is permanently in effect. A rule will only be used if its value is '1'.

The procedure used in Pseudo-Algol may be written:

```
PROCEDURE INFER (FACT)
FOR ALL RULES CONTAINING FACT DO
      IF RULE ACTIVE THEN
            IF FACT VALUE IN RULE = VALUE(FACT)
                  THEN ELIMINATE RULE
                        OTHERWISE VALUE(RULE) = VALUE(RULE) − 1
      FI
      FI
OD
FOR ALL RULES CONTAINING FACT DO
      IF RULE ACTIVE THEN
            NOTE RULE; (* SEE FREE SEARCH*)
            IF VALUE(RULE) = 1 THEN
                  CONCLUSION = UNKNOWN ELEMENT OF
                        RULE;
```

> VALUE(CONCLUSION) = VALUE OF
> CONCLUSION IN RULE;
> ELIMINATE RULE;
> INFER (CONCLUSION)

        FI

      FI

OD

END OF PROCEDURE

Backward chaining is somewhat different here because of the internal representation of the rule by a logical formula which ought to be correct. Nevertheless, the problem arises when no goal is reached and we are still trying to verify a particular goal. The system should then ask for the necessary extra information about the askable facts, and for this we would have to consider all the active rules having this goal in their logical formula. We could therefore say that this is the ultimate goal of the rule. In the rule 'P false or Q true or R true' then 'P false', 'Q true', and 'R true' are all possible goals.

For each of these rules indeterminate elements are brought up. We ask the askable ones for the value to 'ask'. This process is repeated for the others.

PROCEDURE RAISE (GOAL)

FOR ALL RULE CONTAINING GOAL **DO**

    IF RULE ACTIVE AND RULE FINISHES WITH GOAL **THEN**

        FOR ALL ELEMENT BELONGING TO RULE **DO**

            IF ELEMENT INDETERMINABLE **THEN**

                IF ELEMENT ASKABLE

                    THEN VALUE (ELEMENT) = T ASK

                    OTHERWISE VERIFY ELEMENT

                FI

            FI

        OD

    FI

OD

END OF PROCEDURE

The system runs through the base of facts and the questions are asked in the order they are met. The user is able to reply 'True' or 'False' or 'Unknown'. Each 'True' or 'False' answer leads to a forward inference.

PROCEDURE ASK

FOR ALL FACT **DO**

    IF FACT TO ASK **THEN**

```
        ASK FACT;
        IF ANSWER = 'TRUE' OR 'FALSE' THEN
                    INFER (FACT)
           FI
     FI
OD
END OF PROCEDURE
```

The inference engine should work in conjunction with the sentence analyser and the knowledge editor.

The LAURIE system corresponds to the preceding inference engine with a base of some 104 rules to be applied in the case of the breakdown of a twin cylinder motor. It is implemented on APPLE II in Pascal. Here we put forward three dialogues between L (Laurie) and U (User).

U: The gears are slipping.
L: ...
U: The gear lever won't move.
L: Return spring broken on gear lever?
U: Confirmed.

U: The ignition is weak.
L: Damp suppressor?
U: Why?
L: True deduction by the rule:
    If true problem ignition
      and damp spark plug false
      then damp suppressor true.
U: Why is the spark plug not damp?
L: False deduction from the rule:
    If weak ignition true
    then ignition true.
U: Weak ignition?
L: Confirmed true.
U. ...
L: Damp suppressor?
U: False.
L: Suppressor casing damp?
U: Why?
L: True prediction by the rule:
    If true problem ignition
      and damp suppressor false
    then damp suppressor casing true.

U: The gears are slipping.
L: . . .
U: The gear lever won't move.
L. Return spring broken on gear lever?
U: Unknown.
L. Gears stick on deceleration?
U: Yes.
L: Return spring broken on gear lever.

5.2 An inference engine in first-order logic

The introduction of variables into the production rules raises a crucial problem at the inference engine level. It is the threat of entering an endless loop in the choice of the rule (it could be chosen a great many times) and of the instantiation of the rule's variables: point B in the base cycle shown in Fig. 5.2.

We will not be dealing with the problem of the choice of rule here for which a large control structure has been put forward:

- Choice by evaluation: the first rule met in Waterman (1970) or PROLOG where the major priority is the interest relating to that goal which has a priority related to what is considered to be the most important fact. The choice of rule which is most specific as seen in LISP, etc.
- Exhaustive research.
- Metarules have control over what seems to be the best solution.

Here we will study the instantiation of the variables within rules in more detail. Indeed, if five variables exist in one rule and the system is aware at this precise moment of about one hundred facts then we have to look at 100^5 potential attempts in order to evaluate this one rule. Moreover, the order in which the premises of each rule may be evaluated must vary according to the context—following the passage, data, and questions asked. These will make up the different pieces of information which will be known once we try to put a precise rule into operation.

Dynamic order—in which it would be more convenient to evaluate the premises in order to find the n-tuplet of 'matching' variables as quickly as possible—depends on the context and it only the system, at a given moment, which is able to work out a suitable order. Intuitively it is a question of spreading out the known facts, taking into account the restraints which are linked to the base of facts in order to avoid as many choices as possible (and thus useless backtracks).

The procedure adopted in SIMMIAS (Laurière and Perrot, 1981), and which is also used in SNARK, is close to that which we saw in the problem solver using ALICE, but in a completely different field (Laurière, 1978).

We are going to develop the two main points: the process of putting a rule into operation and the process of giving a dynamic order to the premises when the rule is being evaluated. The notations are those used in SNARK as shown in Chapter 4.

Process for putting a rule into operation

For each rule we can work out a collection of key words which characterize it. These are the significant properties or values appearing in the rule (e.g., the YES and NO are not considered to be sufficiently significant as values).

We could say that a rule is impossible to use for a while if one of its key words has a null value in its base of facts. On the other hand, the rule will be labelled as potentially unusable if there are as many, or more, occurrences of its key words as one in the base.

Process for the dynamic ordering of the premises

We always aim to find an n-tuplet of variables as quickly as possible which allows the rule to be put into action and minimizes the number of choices. There was the idea of determining types within premises, which became possible by means of a standard form of expression. Only three sorts of premise may be found in each step of evaluation:

Type 1: Attribute $(x) = a$
   We try to instantiate a floating variable x of which the attribute is a.
Type 2: Attribute $(\$a) = (y)$
   We try to instantiate a floating variable whatever the value of attribute $(\$a)$ may be. The floating variable $a could be the result of the propagation of a choice or an earlier instantiation.
Type 3: Attribute $(x) = (y)$
   The choice of variables to instantiate becomes a function of the type.

The most constrained types take priority: Type 1, then Type 2, and finally Type 3 if these are all that remain. In the case of equality between premises it is the maximum number of occurrences of property within the base of facts which decides.

We run through the base of facts by chaining the value or attribute. We can locate the first suitable object, if there is one, and then add others to this as they occur.

The choice we make is echoed in all the premises which have not yet been evaluated and also on the action section. The implications which this brings about (instantiations and possible changes in the type of premise) are taken into account at the time of the iteration which follows.

In the case of a contradiction with the base of facts or absence of choice we go back and examine the last choice. There is a definitive failure for the current rule when no choice remains at the first level.

There is a definitive success when an n-tuplet of variables has been found and all the premises have been evaluated. In this last case the system memorizes this n-tuplet in order to be prepared later on to send the same rule to another sequence.

Other strategies in evaluating a rule of first-order logic are possible; see TANGO (Cordier and Rousset, 1982) and ALOUETTE (Mulet-Marquis, 1983).

Let us finish with a few remarks on programming languages for expert systems.

Classically, LISP is considered to be the programming language of artificial intelligence. The example in Sec. 5.1.2 seems to confirm this. On examining the example in more detail this advantage does not appear to be quite so great for at least two reasons:

1. If we make the structure of the facts and rules more complex then LISP loses its legibility and we find ourselves forced to create an interface between the internal representation of LISP and the face it presents to the user.

   This, to the author's mind, is the essential reason for having interfaces in natural language, as are found in all the expert systems written in LISP. An example of this is the BAOBAB interface for MYCIN.
2. A certain slowness in the execution of programs written in LISP which does not allow us to make use of LISP machines effectively.

The new language of artificial intelligence today seems to be PROLOG. It appears to be completely suitable for writing expert systems as it contains its own first-order logic inference engine. The fact that it allows, by simple formalization, simultaneously to describe and solve problems is certainly one of the reasons for it to have been chosen by the Japanese as the prototype for future languages. In spite of these preceding serious points the advantages of PROLOG, as it stands at the moment, do not seem to be much in advance of LISP.

It certainly seems that we still have to define a language which is based on first-order logic, like PROLOG, and which has the characteristics which make it easy to read and operate, as with SNARK. The languages such as PL/1 and Pascal could then be the languages which support future expert systems.

To conclude this short debate on support languages there are two final comments. One is theoretical and the other is practical.

From a theoretical point of view we can certainly confirm that a tree type of data structure, which is the basis of LISP and PROLOG, is not the best choice. The recent results of J. Corbin and M. Bidiot (1983) could be pushed forward on the strength of this thesis. The authors show that Robinson's algorithm of unification which was, until now, exponential (by using a tree structure for the data) is in fact of quadratic form (by using a graph type of diagram for the data).

From the practical point of view the most general first-order logic inference engines are not often written in LISP. SNARK is written in PL/1 and in Pascal. ALOUETTE is written in Pascal and GOSSEYN (Fouet and colleagues, 1983) is written in FORTRAN.

6. The areas of application of expert systems

In practice, the difference between the 'expert system approach' and the 'classic approach' is as follows:

- On the one hand, the types of problems to be solved.
- On the other hand, the way in which the problems are to be solved.

Indeed, expert systems are particularly well adapted for the resolution of certain sorts of problems where:

- A great quantity of information is provided.
- The collection of pieces of information is not fixed, but progressive.
- These pieces of information are rather of the heuristic than algorithmic type, although the use of algorithms is not excluded.
- The symbolic treatment of the information leads to as numeric treatment although numeric treatments may not be excluded.
- A qualitative analysis of the problem and its context has a much, if not more, importance as its quantitative analysis.
- The path taken in order to come to a solution is just as important as the solution itself.

These properties reveal the principal characteristics of the expert systems which follow:

1. Those which concern the knowledge base.
   (a) It contains a great amount of information.
   (b) These pieces of information are complex and have many uses.
   (c) It contains pieces of information about the use of these pieces of information (metaknowledge).
   (d) The pieces of information are stored in modular and declarative forms and as independent modules.
   (e) The knowledge base is not static, but cumulative.
2. Those concerned with the problem-solving system.
   (a) A problem is solved 'step by step' and each step corresponds to a stage in the solution process.

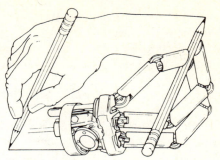

Fig. 6.1   The man–machine interface

(b) Each stage in the solution process is (or can be) explained (e.g., in the way it is carried out having a clear semantic representation in the face of the problem being solved).
(c) The strategy for solving problems is not static, but can be dynamic according to the problem and its context.
(d) The user may intervene in the solving process by guiding the system by strategies and his/her own heuristics.

Two essential qualities come out of this:

1. The possibility of a relaxed man–machine conversation.
2. The system's capacity for intelligent and intelligible reasoning.

These two basic characteristics clearly define the appropriate areas for this application. They are all the areas where an intelligent interactive system is necessary.

We will now look at the main areas and make a purely arbitrary breakdown into:

– Systems which help
– Teaching aids
– Problem solving

6.1 Systems which help

6.1.1 Diagnostic aids

The classical systems are those which help diagnosis, especially medical diagnosis.

Notable in this area are:

– MYCIN (Shortliffe, 1976) to help decisions regarding bacterial blood infections (200 rules in propositional logic), BAOBAB (Bonnet, 1979) and TEISERIAS (Davis, 1979) complete the group.

- CASNET (Weiss and colleagues, 1976) to help the diagnosis of glaucoma of the eye. Possessing a model of glaucoma which allows us to follow its progress.
- Fouet (1983) puts forward a project which helps large programs to be maintained.
- INTERNIST (Pople and colleagues, 1975) deals with diagnosis in internal medicine. The system carries several million rules separated into 80 subject groups. Large numbers of fields of study and human ailments have already been coded by several dozen specialists.
- PUFF (Feigenbaum, 1977) for the diagnosis of lung infections.
- HEADMED (Rychener, 1976) specializing in pharmacological treatment in psychiatry.
- ONCOCIN (Shortliffe *et al.*, 1981) is a system which is being written to help with the treatment of cancer.
- VM (Feigenbaum, 1979) is a help system for resuscitating patients. It receives the signals directly from the various clinical sensors, watches their development continuously and sets off an alarm at the sign of any serious anomaly.
- SAM (Gascuel, 1981) is a system which was conceived at the Salpétrière to help the diagnosis of brain haemorrhages (35 rules) and with choosing a course of treatment for high blood pressure (200 rules).
- SPHINX (Fieschi and colleagues, 1982) is a system which helps decision making in the world of medicine and was conceived in the Medical Department of the University of Marseilles.
- DART (Bennett and Hollander, 1981) is a 'consultant' for breakdowns in equipment or systems (initialization, user connection in timesharing). The rules are essentially the translation of communications protocols and possible anomalies. An IBM product.
- Parcy (1982) puts forward a pre-prototype expert system to help monitor fast atomic reactors.

6.1.2 Aids to design and manufacture

A second group of systems of note are those which help with design and construction. They are expected to go further than the current CAD/CAM systems by posing solutions to the operator.

In this field we have:

- SACON (Bennett and colleagues, 1978) which controls a program for structural analysis from a strategic point of view.

- TROPIC (Latcombe, 1977) is a general help program for designing in both architecture and electrical transformers.
- GARI (Descottes, 1981) which gives more details about manufacturing scales starting from advice given by specialists (50 rules).
- EL (Sussman, 1975) and NASL (McDermott, 1978) helping with electrical circuit design.
- NUDGE (Goldstein and Roberts, 1977) for the elaboration of time management especially when the problem is not completely specified.
- MOLGEN (Friendland, 1979) to help in the field of genetic experiments. From different 'tools' which are known to be able to cut, link, insert, and kill molecules of DNA. With the known effects of such modifications and by the state of chemical technology, it is always a problem to decide, for a specific genetic goal, where to start and how to get there.
- RITA (Anderson and Gillogly, 1976) is a way of help with conception.
- R1 (McDermott, 1981) to study the configuration of a computer. It was written in the OPS language by a team of fifteen using 850 rules. It proposes complete configurations for VAX 11 systems (Digital Equipment Corp.) which satisfy a group of constraints which have been imposed on such things as total space available, distance, positions of controllers and clients' specifications.
- PECOS (Barstow, 1979) translates abstract algorithms for the manipulation of symbols, graphs and arithmetic into LISP (400 rules).
- (Bocquet, 1982) for reading and understanding industrial drawings.

This impressive list must not, however, lead us to be overoptimistic. Most of the systems are experimental and not widely used. It is just that these prototype systems do not have all the qualities required by an ideal system, as defined at the start of this section. Moreover, as we will see in Chapter 7, the transfer of expertise from man to machine is neither straightforward nor easy.

However, some prototype implementations do exist and the applications of this approach to expert systems are possible in the industrial field just as they are in that of diagnosis, guidance, and maintenance, as in the study of reliability and computer-aided design (see Gondran and Laleuf, 1983).

6.2 Teaching aids

This is a wide field for an expert system thanks to its two essential characteristics of dialogue and intelligent behaviour. Traditional lessons helped by computer (CAI, computer-aided instruction) have one of the following characteristics:

- Either they are incapable of solving the problems which they ask the

student, as they possess one answer which is programmed into them as the one and only answer.
- Or, if they are able, they do it with the help of algorithms which are incapable of being broken down into human terms and as a result have been adapted in a way which is hardly suitable for teaching.

They are mostly closed systems, unable to reply to a pupil's question. The expert system has knowledge of that which it is teaching. Regardless of the fact that a pupil can ask it questions the expert system provides two academic advantages:

- It allows the pupil to be followed step by step, when the teacher would not be able to do so. Sometimes a pupil finds a new way of doing something and the teacher fails to notice it and believes a mistake has been made.
- In the case of an expert system you can introduce false rules and deviations from rules which correspond to the habitual mistakes made by pupils. The system is able to understand when the pupil makes a mistake, guide him/her and suggest remedial exercises.

Now, in spite of the examples which will shortly be quoted there is no CAI package which is truly operational and based on expert systems. We should realize that the traditional CAI form of instruction has become rather old-fashioned. Things are going to change since the expert system approach forces one to think deeply about education. Some authors now refer to ICAI (intelligent computer-aided instruction) and we can refer to several early results in this field.

- LOGO (Papert, 1970) allows children to express their ideas freely using a machine. Papert is currently one of the 'Popes' of microcomputing in the World Computer Centre!
- SCHOLAR (Carbonell, 1970) was the first one to put explicit knowledge about the subject to be taught (the geography of South America) so that it was capable of inferring between different facts ('Does Guyana produce rubber?'). An answer to this could be, 'I don't think so, but Peru is in South America and it produces rubber' and to sustain a conversation of 'shared initiative' with the student.
- SOPHIE (Brown and Burton, 1975) is a computer teaching aid which is used to detect breakdowns in electrical circuits.
- BUGGY (Brown and Burton, 1978) is an experimental system which is centred on the errors made by students. The authors clearly showed that errors of calculation came in fact from incorrect methods which had been used systematically by the students.

– GUIDON (Clancey, 1979) is a teaching system which is designed for medical students at Stanford and is based on the rules of MYCIN.

In the article of Stevens, Collins, and Goldin (1979) we can find a classification of students' errors due to the limitation of the field (and thus due to oversimplification), overgeneralization, overdifferentiation (considering the factors as necessary for an inference when they are not so), and errors of reasoning (coming to a conclusion when all the premises have not been verified). Then we will quote a number of syntheses of ICAI, Bonnett (1980), and the papers delivered at the ICAI Symposium AFCET-Informatique, 1981. ICAI seems to be the field with the biggest future in it.

We should note that the bases of knowledge needed by ICAI are just the same as those for the necessary bases of knowledge for helping with problems which are connected with it. There should, therefore, be a strong interaction between these two approaches.

The structure of an ICAI system has been presented by Bonnett, Cordier, and Kayser (1981) and Rousset and Cordier (1982), where you have a clear distinction between what is being taught and the teaching strategy. Just as with the subject you are teaching, the strategy of teaching can be explained by means of the production rules.

The ICAI system is made up of an expert module, a teaching module, and a machine–student interface module, as shown in Fig. 6.2.

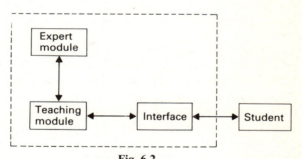

Fig. 6.2

The teaching module controls the dialogue with the student by explicitly using pedagogic rules of the following types:

If the student's reply communicated by the interface is judged to be false by the expert module and if the student used a correct method, then the module decides to ask for more details. In order to effect this conversation it uses the interface module for everything which is to do with man–machine communication. It can also, at any time, call the expert module for all the information which is connected with this field in order to evaluate the student's reply, generate a problem with a given difficulty, identify errors, etc. Finally, in order that it might adapt itself to each student the teaching module produces a student profile and continually consults it.

6.3 Problem solving

6.3.1 Recognition of forms

An important area is that of the recognition of forms. We can quote from the following:

- DENDRAL (Feigenbaum, Buchanan, and Lederberg, 1971) identifies an organic substance from its basic formula and mass spectrograph. The structure of the program is interesting for it mixes production rules and data provided by a simulation. A 'generator' based on rules of production suggests those formulae which are possible in principle. A 'planner' based on very specialized chemical knowledge governed by rules allows the number of created cases to be considerably reduced by the 'generator' as a result. A 'predictor' simulates mass spectrographs from the remaining cases as a result. Finally, the rules of production allow the comparison of spectrographs which were determined in this way with the true ones. So for di-n-decyl ($C_{20}H_{42}$) there were more than 11 million possible cases; the planner only allowed 22 366 cases simulated by the 'predictor' to be examined.

  It is a system which is used daily by chemists at Stanford and we could cite several reasons for its success. Firstly there is the quality of the authors, especially Lederberg (Nobel Prize for Medicine), who had since 1964 used a methodology to help with organic chemical analysis. So in this field it is applied by the use of simulation in conjunction with the production rules. It was in fact completely rewritten from a procedural program of the conventional type.
- METADENDRAL (Buchanan and Feigenbaum, 1978) automatically infers rules for fragmentation of molecules which are used for DENDRAL.
- PROSPECTOR (Konolige, 1979) is a system which helps in mining prospecting.
- DIPMETER (Davis *et al.*, 1981) reconstitutes the real nature and the position of geological layers from the analysis of physical signs ('logs') which have risen through the subsoil. It is written in EMYCIN and is made up from the extraction procedures derived from the significant forms of the signs.

- LITHO (Bonnet, 1981) is similar to the previous system. It was written at Schlumberger and contains 400 rules.
- SIMMIAS (Laurière and Perrot, 1981) is also a system to help in oil prospecting. It is written in SNARK and contains about 100 rules.
- CRYSALIS (Englemore and Terry, 1979) determines the structure of proteins from three-dimensional electron density cards which come from X-ray crystallographic analysis.

6.3.2 Robotics

Another area is the use of expert systems in robotics. At present artificial intelligence has made little impact on robotics other than at an experimental level in some research centres. Such robots as Herman (introduced at TMI), Virgule and its descendants (used at The Hague), Mam (which climbs a wall with the aid of suction pads and can inspect soldered joints by weaving a way through pipes), and Mis (which inspects the inside of atomic reactors) are telemanipulators. The efforts of researchers are now turned towards the autonomy of robots. They are designing sensors sensitive to light, sound, and touch and at the same time are improving the qualities of information processing. It is here, for these third-generation robots, that expert systems can make a contribution. We can distinguish three levels: that of the communication between the robot and the operator, through the treatment of natural languages in particular; that of perception and analysis of a scene or evolved vision; that of the action of the robot through the possibility of special reasoning.

There are a number of fields of research at present:

- SHDRLU (Winograd, 1972) is a conversational program in natural language between a human operator and a robot which manipulates very simple geometrical shapes.
- The WAVE languages (Stanford University, 1970), AL (Finkel, 1974), and AUTOPASS (Lieberman, 1977) are languages for manipulation or mechanical assembly.
- SHAKEY (Stanford University, 1970) is the first robot, topped by a roving-eye television camera and a telemeter, which finds its way around a room full of boxes. It pushes these boxes around and stacks them in a given place. As for its successors JASON (Berkeley University) and SYNTELMANN (Kleinwachter at Lorrach, Germany), the work on SHAKEY has been abandoned after several years of experiments.

This research was picked up in France using microelectronics in the HILAIRE project (Laboratoire d'Automatique et d'Analyse des Systèmes du CRNS in Toulouse with the support of Laboratoire Langages et

Systèmes at Toulouse University). However, for the moment it seems that robots are in the category of 'intelligent, but useless'.
- ARGOS II (Cayrol, Fade, and Farreny, 1979) is an expert system which is directed towards the control of third-generation robots. Like HILAIRE it consists of a generator of plans of action and a monitor to execute them.

6.3.3 Games

A rapidly expanding field in the use of expert systems is that of games. To give examples there are:

- Waterman's program (1970) for playing poker. The rules are in this case based on probabilities, giving the program an excellent performance.
- PARADISE (Wilkins, 1979) for the game of chess.
- Quinlan's programs (1979) and those of Popescu (1982) for bridge playing.

6.3.4 Automatic demonstration of theorems

A field which remains at the base of all research into expert systems is that of the automatic demonstration of theorems. For example we have:

- PARI (Bourgouin, 1978) which handles arithmetic problems.
- Pastre's programs (1978) and those of Marialdo (1979) which demonstrate several hundred group theory theorems.
- AM (Lenat, 1977) 'discovers' mathematical concepts. Using elementary concepts the program is able to generate new concepts and judge their appropriateness by using the production rules. The field in which this may be applied is huge. It would be interesting to translate the ALICE (Laurière, 1979) general system, which solves combined problems, into an expert system. An important application would be the research into a database; see Siklossy and Laurière, 1982.

7. Past and future of expert systems

7.1 The past

The representation of knowledge in the form of production rules does not date from yesterday. We could say that right from the birth of the written word man has used production rules to structure knowledge. The oldest medical document which has been found is an example of this. According to Edwin Smith (Breasted, 1930), it is all found on a papyrus of the seventeenth century BC which corresponds to a copy of a work belonging to the ancient Egyptian Empire at the beginning of the third millenium. This famous piece of text presents 48 surgical observations regarding head wounds and all use the same formal representation of: title, examination, diagnosis, and treatment.

The examination/diagnosis pair is always presented in the form of: 'If you examine a man who has a certain symptom . . ., you will say about him: it is this illness. . . .' The prognosis follows, whether favourable, uncertain, or fatal, which translates, according to the case, by one of three formulae: 'It is a pain that I will treat . . .', 'It is a pain that I will beat . . .', 'It is a pain that I can do nothing for. . .'.

Figure 7.1 shows the seventeenth observation.

Besides medical manuscripts we have found numerous knowledge bases with a very strong structure in other ancient literature. Without doubt the most common are those books of divinatory recipes or the interpretation of dreams. For example, the ninth century book about the interpretation of the Duke of Tcheou's dreams (Drège, 1981) presents more than three hundred production rules in the following form:

- Dream that you are rising towards the sky: you will become a high ranking public official and you will receive money and splendour.
- Dream that you are falling into water: worries with your wife or the tax man.
- Dream that fire and water destroy your house: disaster or moving house.
- Dream that you are falling into latrines: sign of dangerous illness.

Title
Instructions for looking af
a fractured cheek bone

Examination
If you examine a man wit
a fractured cheek bone yo
will find red protruding
inflammation around
the wound.

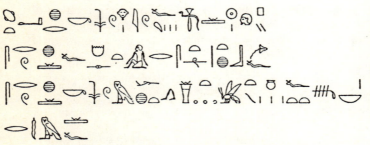

Diagnosis and prognosis
You tell the patient,
'This is a fracture of the
cheek bone.
It is an illness I can treat.'

Treatment
You will dress it with fres
meat on the first day.
The treatment will last
until the swelling is
reduced. Then you will
cure it with strawberries
honey, and bandages
which must be changed
daily until he is cured.

Fig. 7.1

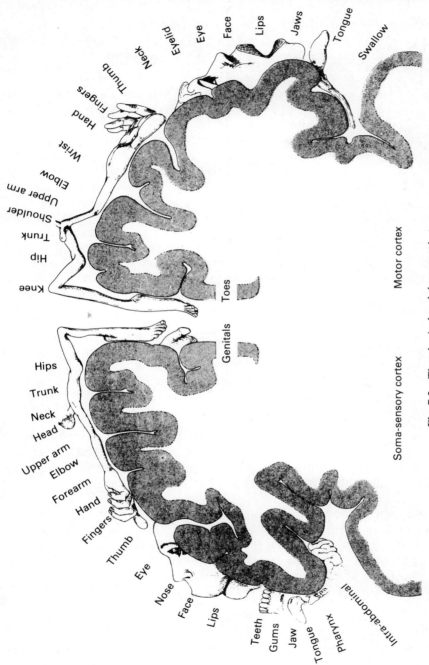

Fig. 7.2 The physical and the mental

- Dream that your wife is happy: obtaining someone's possessions.
- Dream that husband and wife are holding hands: very disastrous.
- Dream that your wife is wearing lots of makeup: certain separation.

These bases of knowledge are only sure at a certain level and really only allow a game of direct question and answer. However, their size is often important, more important than the knowledge base used by a large number of the expert systems mentioned in Chapter 6.

In respect of their illustrious precursors, expert systems have to concentrate on trying to overcome certain walls of complexity. The first wall of complexity is linked to the quantity of knowledge. In the case of knowledge linked with the rules of propositional logic it seems that it would not be too difficult to get over this wall. The second wall of complexity is connected with a more important structure of our knowledge. These pieces of knowledge correspond rather to first-order logic and the wall of complexity will be more difficult to overcome. The difference between current databases will be important.

Let us end this look at the past by trying to understand why most of the current expert systems are hardly used. It is the belief of the author that they just have not yet reached this wall of complexity. They are not particularly interesting for a specialist and are too clever for the general user. They give us, in fact, no more than Smith's papyrus!

7.2 The future

Artificial intelligence through expert systems has today reached an operational stage with very promising evidence for its continued use. Two facts seem to be important:

1. Knowledge bases will completely revolutionize the storage of information. Computer systems are going to become really intelligent and the time seems close when the Turing test will be positive: 'The user will not be able to distinguish whether the being which is answering him via the terminal is a man or a machine.'
2. The conversation between man and machine no longer calls for the intervention of a computer programmer. It will no longer be necessary for the user to write a program to solve a problem, but only to specify the problem in a language which is more formal than natural language (see the example in Chapter 4 for diagnosis). The problem of reliability of the logic will be resolved in this way.

It seems, therefore, that a true revolution is happening under our noses. Is the place of man in the Universe going to be called into question for a third time after Copernicus and Darwin? Today it is his intelligence which is being questioned. Are we far away from the HAL computer of *2001, A Space Odyssey*?

The Japanese have certainly predicted this revolution by putting forward the MITI report of 1981 on fifth-generation computers, even leaving out the publicity aspect.

But today we are still not quite there. After the failure of automatic translation in the sixties we should have more modest aims. Indeed, we would need a great amount of knowledge to be able to reach a goal which was not so hard to achieve. The constitution of the knowledge base belonging to specialists in this field poses at least two questions. The first is of a theoretical nature.

It is not always possible to explain a behavioural rule and the search for such rules places a restriction on psychoanalysis. Claude Bernard sums this difficulty up in the following lines:

Nous pouvons plus que nous savons,
Nous savions plus que nous ne comprenons,
Nous comprenons plus que nous ne pouvons expliquer.

(We can do more than we know, we know more than we understand, we understand more than we are able to explain.)

Already we find this difficulty in a number of ancient texts:

'L'écrit ne peut pas exprimer entièrement les paroles. Les paroles ne peuvent pas exprimer complètement les pensées,' the Master in the Yi King tells us. (Writings cannot completely explain words. Words cannot completely explain thoughts.)

The second question is of a deontological nature since there could well be theft of expert knowledge among computer systems. It is the author's opinion that, as far as technical problems go, there is quite a satisfactory answer to this. It is enough to cite the author of each rule as would happen in a review article. This solution allows us to be more successful in bringing up the knowledge base and bibliography which sustains it. Finally, and above all, the expert system will have the quality of a knowledge base. In fact, outside of computer science problems, it is by the quality of the knowledge base that most of the expert systems are judged. It is not with indifference to the author to report that the most frequently used expert system, DENDRAL, is based on a methodology using a structure of knowledge (in a restricted field) produced by a Nobel Prize winner, Lederberg.

The future of expert systems depends on their construction by man and his knowledge. It is comforting to think that it is not solely a technical or computer adventure but above all an adventure resulting from the application of human intelligence and teamwork.

Bibliography

Anderson, R. and J. Gillogly (1976). 'Rand intelligent terminal agent RITA design and philosophy', R, 1809, ARPA.

Barstow, D. R. (1979). 'An experiment in knowledge based automatic programming', *Artificial Intelligence*, **12**, 73–119.

Bennet, J. S. and C. R. Hollander (1981). 'DART: an expert system for computer fault diagnosis', *International Joint Conference on Artificial Intelligence*, pp. 843–845.

Bocquet, J. C. (1981). 'Reconstitution automatique d'une représentation tridimensionnelle à factor d'un dessin industriel', Thèse 3ᵉ cycle, Université Paris 6, October.

Bonnet, A. (1979). 'BAOBAB: a parser for a rule-based system using a semantic grammar', Stanford University technical report HPP 78–10.

Bonnet, A. (1980). 'De l'application de l'Intelligence Artificielle à l'enseignement assisté par ordinateur: l'EIAO', Colloque sur quelques méthodes en Intelligence Artificielle, Publications du GR 22 CNRS, Caen.

Bonnet, A., M. O. Cordier, and D. Kayser (1981). 'An ICAI system for teaching derivatives in mathematics', WCEE 81, July 81, Lausanne.

Breasted, J. (1930). *The Edwin Smith Surgical Papyrus*, Chicago, 1930 (Bibliothèque d'Egyptologie du Collège de France).

Brown, J. S. and R. Burton (1975). 'Multiple representations of knowledge for tutorial reasoning', in Bobrow and Collins (eds), *Representation and Understanding*, Academic Press, New York.

Brown, J. S. and R. Burton (1978). 'Diagnostic models for procedural bugs in basic mathematical skills', *Cognitive Science*, **2**, 155–192.

Buchanan, B. and E. Feigenbaum (1978). 'DENTRAL and METADENTRAL', *Artificial Intelligence*, **11**, 5–24.

Bundy, A., *et al.* (1979). 'Solving mechanics problems using meta-level inference', *Proc. International Joint Conference on Artificial Intelligence*, **6**, 1017–1027.

Carbonell, J. (1970). 'AI in CAI, An artificial intelligence approach to computer-assisted instruction', *IEEE Transactions on man-machine systems*, vol. MMS, December.

Cayrol, M., B. Fade, and H. Farreny (1979). 'Objets formels et liaisons d'attributs dans Argos II', *Second Congrès AFCET de Reconnaissance des Formes et Intelligence Artificielle*, Toulouse.

Charniak, E. (1978). 'On the use of frame knowledge', *Artificial Intelligence*, **11**, 3, 225–266.

Chomsky, N. (1965). *Aspects of the Theory of Syntax*, MIT Press, Cambridge, Mass.

Clancey, W. 'Tutoring rules for guiding a case method dialogue', *International Journal of Man–Machine Studies*, **11**, 25–49.

Colmerauer, A. (1977). 'La programmation en logique du premier ordre', Actes Journées IRIA *La Compréhension*.

Corbin, J., and M. Bidoit (1983). 'A rehabilitation of Robinson's unification algorithm', *Proc. IFIP 9th World Computer Congress*, North-Holland, pp. 904–914.

Cordier, M. O. (1979). '*Commande d'un robot en langage naturel dans un domaine nécessitant des connaissances pragmatiques: les recette de cuisine*', Thèse 3e cycle, LRI Paris XI.

Cordier, M. O. and M. C. Rousset (1982). 'TANGO-moteur d'inférences pour un Système-Expert variables', Publication du GR 22 No. 30, Utilisation de connaissances déclaratives, pp. 83–117.

Davis, R. (1977). 'Interactive transfer of expertise: Acquisition of new infference rules', *Proc. International Joint Conference on Artificial Intelligence*, **5**, p. 321–328.

Davis, R., H. Austin, I. Carlbom, B. Frawley, P. Pruchnick, R. Sneiderman, and J. A. Gilreath (1981). 'The DIPMETER advisor: interpretation of geological signals', *International Joint Conference on Artificial Intelligence*, **7**, 846–849.

Demonchaux, E. (1981). 'Représentation des connaissances et stratégie d'évaluation des règles dans un Système Expert', Publication du GR 22, Colloque d'Intelligence Artificielle de Toulouse, pp. 101–124.

Descottes, Y. (1981). 'GARI un système expert pour la conception des gammes d'usinage', Thèse 3e cycle, IMAG, Grenoble 1.

Dincbas, M. (1980). 'Le système de résolution de problème METALOG', Rapport CERT/DERI, No. 3146 convention DRET 79.1216, Toulouse.

Drège, J. P. (1981). 'Clefs des songes de Toueng-Houang', in *Nouvelles Contributions aux Études de Toueng-Houang*, Centre de Recherches d'Histoire et de Philosophie, Librairie Droz, Genève, pp. 205–249.

Duda, R. O. (1982). 'The PROSPECTOR consultation system', Final Report SRI 8172.

Dumont, J. and C. Schuster (1982). *Jouer à Raisonner*, Les Éditions d'Organisation, Paris.

Engelmore, R. and A. Terry (1979). 'Structure and function of the CRYSALIS System', *Proc. International Joint Conference on Artificial Intelligence*, **6**, 250–256.

Feigenbaum, E. (1971). 'On generality and problem solving: DENDRAL', *Machine Intelligence*, **6**, 165–190.

Feigenbaum, E. (1977). 'The art of artificial intelligence', *Proc. International Joint Conference on Artificial Intelligence*, **5**, 1014–1029.

Feigenbaum, E. A., B. G. Buchanan, and J. Lederberg (1971). 'On generality, and problem solving: A case study using the DENDRAL program'. In B. Meltzer and D. Michie (eds), *Machine Intelligence*, vol. 6. Edinburgh University Press, pp. 165–190.

Fieschi, M. (1983). 'SPHINX: un Système Expert d'aide à la décision en médecine', Thèse de Doctorat d'État en Biologie Humaine, Faculté de Médecine de l'Université d'Aix-Marseille II.

Fieschi, M., M. Joubert, D. Fieschi, G. Botti, R. Bruchet, M. Roux, B. Monges and J. Salducci (1982). 'Présentation d'un système expert d'aide à la décision en Médecine: SPHINX, *Journées d'études AFCET sur les systèmes experts*, Avignon.

Finkel, R. *et al.* (1974). *AL Programming System for Automation,*—STANCS 74-456—Stanford University.

Fouet, J. M., A. Aquesbi, J. C. Bocquet, S. Tichkiewitch, M. Reynier, and P. Trau (1983). 'An expert system for computer aided mechanical design', *Proc. IFIP 9th World Computer Congress*, North-Holland, pp. 121–125.

Friedland, P. (1979). 'Knowledge-based experiment design in molecular genetics', *Proc. International Joint Conference on Artificial Intelligence*, **6**, 285–288.

Gallaire, H. and J. Minker (1978). *Logic and Data Bases*, Plenum Pub. Corp., New York.

Gardin, J. C. (1979). *Une Archéologie Théorique*, Hachette, Paris.

Gardin, J. C. and M. S. Lagrange (1975). 'Essais d'analyse du discours archéologique', Notes et Monographies Techniques du Centre de Researches Archéologiques No. 7, Editions du CNRS, Paris.

Gascuel, O. (1981). 'Un programme général d'aide à la décision médicale structurant automatiquement ses connaissances', Congrès ARCET-RFIA, Nancy.

Goldstein, I. and R. Roberts (1977). (NUDGE: a knowledge based scheduling program', *Proc. International Joint Conference on Artificial Intelligence*, **5**, 257–263.

Gondran, M. and M. Minoux (1979). *Graphes et Algorithmes*, Eyrolles.

Gondran, M., and J. C. Laleuf (1983). La représentation des connaissances en fiabilité, note EDF HI 4600/02.

Gondran, M., and J. C. Laleuf (1984). 'La représentation des connaissances ces dans les études de fialilité: l'analyse F.C.P.', note EDF–DER HI 4600/02 (1983). In Congress IFDRS, *Operational Research '84* J.C. Brans (ed.), North-Holland, pp. 112–123.

Gondran, M., J. F. Hery, J. C. Laleuf (1984). 'Un système expert prototype sur la conduite en fonctionnement normal d'une centrale PWR', note EDF–DER.

Konolige, K. (1979). 'An inference net compiler for the PROSPECTOR rule-based consultation system', *Proc. International Joint Conference on Artificial Intelligence*, **6**, 487–489.

Lagrange, M. S. and M. Renaud (1982). 'Simulation d'un raisonnement archéologique—Description de l'application d'un système expert = le système SNARK', Document de Travail No. 1 du LISH.

Latombe, J. C. (1977). 'Une application de l'intelligence artificielle à la conception assistée par ordinateur', Thèse d'État, Grenoble.

Lauière, J. L. (1978). 'A language for stating and solving combinatorial problems', *Artificial Intelligence*, **10**, 2, 29–127.

Laurière, J. L. (1979). 'Changement de représentation en résolution de problèmes', Actes de la journée AFCET les représentations graphiques de l'information.

Laurière, J. L. (1982a). 'La programmation sans instruction: l'approche des systèmes experts', Actes du Colloque AFCET *Mathématiques de l'Informatique*, pp. 31–40.

Laurière, J. L. (1982b). 'Représentation et utilisation des connaissances, 1e partie: les systèmes experts', Technique et Science Informatique No. 1, 2e partie; 'Représentations de Connaissances', Technique et Science Informatiques No. 2.

Laurière, J. L. (1982c). 'Le système SNARK: symbolic normalized acquisition and representation of knowledge', Rapport Institut de Programmation 427.

Laurière, J. L. (1984). *Intelligence Artificielle: Résolutions de Problèmes par l'Homme et la Machine* (à paraître).

Laurière, J. L. and A. Perrot (1981). 'Représentation et utilisation de connaissances dans l'industrie pétrolière', Journées d'Études AFCET sur les systèmes experts, Avignon.

Lenat, D. (1977). 'The ubiquity of discovery', *Artificial Intelligence*, **9**, 3, 257–286.

Lewis Carrol (1896). *La Logique sans Peine*, Hermann, Paris, 1982.

Lopez, M. (1979). 'Rèalisation d'un interface de communication en langue naturelle avec le système TROPIC', *Congrès AFCET*, Toulouse, pp. 25–35.

McDermott, D. (1978). 'Planning and acting', *Cognitive Science*, **2**, 71–109.

McDermott, J. (1982). 'R1: A rule based configurer of Computer Systems', *Artificial Intelligence*, **19**, 39–88.

Marquant, C. (1982). 'LAURIE, langage d'aide à l'utillisateur et à la recherche d'Informations Expertes', rapport de DEA, Université de Paris 6, Professeur J. L. Laurière.

Mulet-Marquis, D. (1983). 'Intelligence artificielle: quelques exemples d'utilisation du moteur d'inférence Alouette', *Bulletin du Centre de Calcul des Études et Recherches EDF*.

Nii, N. (1978). 'Rules bases understanding of signal'. In *Pattern Directed Inference Systems*.

Papert, S. (1970). 'Teaching children programming', *IFIP Conference on Computer Education*, Amsterdam, North-Holland.

Parcy, J. P. (1982). 'Un système expert en diagnostic sur réacteurs à neutrons rapides', Thèse de 3ᵉ cycle, Université de Marseille-Luminy, September.

Pastre, D. (1978). 'Automatic theorem proving in set theory', *Artificial Intelligence*, **10**, 1, 1–27.

Popescur, R. (1982). 'Jeu de la carte au bridge', Publication du GR 22 No. 30, Utilisation de connaissances déclaratives, pp. 339–360.

Pople, H. E., J. D. Myers, and R. A. Miller (1975). 'DIALOG: A model of diagnostic logic for internal medicine', *International Joint Conference on Artificial Intelligence*, **4**, pp. 848–855.

Queinnec, C. (1983). *Language d'un Autre Type: LISP*, Collection Micro-ordinateurs, Eyrolles.

Rousset, M. C. and M. O. Cordier (1982). 'An expert pedagogue for an intelligent CAI system', European Conference on Artificial Intelligence, Orsay.

Roux, J. P. (1971). 'Essai d'interprétation d'un relief figuratif seldjoukide', *Arts Asiatiques*, **XXIII**, 41–49.

Rychener, M. D. (1976). *Production Systems as a Programming Language for Artificial Intelligence Applications*, Ph. D., Carnegie Mellon University, **1** and **2**.

Schank, R. and R. Abelson (1977). *Scripts, Plans, Gools and Understanding*, Laurence Erlbaum associates Inc., Milesdale NJ.

Shortliffe, E. (1976). *MYCIN: Computer Based Medical Consultation*, Elsevier.

Shortliffe, E. H., A. Carlisle Scott, M. B. Bischoff, A. B. Campbelle, W. Van Melle, and C. D. Jacobb. 'ONCOCIN: an expert system for oncology protocol managment', *International Joint Conference on Artificial Intelligence*, **7**, 876–981.

Simmons, R. F. (1973). 'Semantic networks: their computation and use for understanding English sentences', in *Computer Models of Thought and Language*, Schank and Colby (eds), Freeman and Co., San Francisco.

Siklossy, L. and J. L. Laurière (1982). '*Extending the Relational Data Base Model: An Application of Problem Solving Techniques*', American Association for Artificial intelligence, Pittsburgh.

Stefik (1981). 'Planning with constraints: MOLGEN', *Artificial Intelligence*, **16**, 2, 111–140.

Stevens, A., A. Collins, and S. Goldin (1979). 'Misconceptions in student's understanding', *International Journal of Man–Machine Studies*, **11**, 145–156.

Sussman (1975). 'Computer aided circuit analysis', *IEEE, CAS*, **2**, 11, 857–865.

Van Melle, W. (1979). 'A domain independant production rule system for consultation systems', *Proc. International Joint Conference on Artificial Intelligence*, **6**.

Waterman, D. (1970). 'Generalization and learning of heuristics', *Artificial Intelligence*, **1**, 121–170.

Weiss, S., C. A. Kulikowski, M. Trigoboff, and A. Safir (1976). 'Clinical consultation and the representation of disease process: some Artificial Intelligence approaches', *Report CEM-TR 58 Rutgers U.*

Wilkins, D. E. (1979). 'Using plans in chess', *Proc. International Joint Conference on Artificial Intelligence*, **6**, pp. 960–967.

Winston, P. H. and B. K. P. Horn (1981). *LISP*, Addison-Wesley Publishing Company.

Woods, W. A. (1970). 'Transition network grammars for natural language analysis', *Comm. ACM*, **13**, 10, 591–606.